D0984001

Native American Fashion

Modern Adaptations of Traditional Designs

Margaret Wood

Photographs
by DeCastro Studios

Illustrations
by Susan Raudman and Charles Wood

 VAN NOSTRAND REINHOLD COMPANY
New York Cincinnati Toronto London Melbourne

Note: The border design used throughout this book is an authentic Pueblo pottery motif. It, as well as the motifs on pages 9, 27, 32, 49, 67, 74, 91, 104, and 118, are Native American designs that appear in *American Indian Design and Decoration,* by Le Roy H. Appleton (published by Dover Publications, Inc., 1971).

Copyright © 1981 by Van Nostrand Reinhold Company
Library of Congress Catalog Card Number 81-5012
ISBN 0-442-20756-5

Printed in the United States of America
Designed by Ginger Legato
Cover photograph by Jerry Jacka

Published by Van Nostrand Reinhold Company
135 West 50th Street, New York, NY 10020

Van Nostrand Reinhold Limited
1410 Birchmount Road
Scarborough, Ontario M1P 2E7, Canada

Van Nostrand Reinhold Australia Pty. Ltd.
17 Queen Street
Mitcham, Victoria 3132, Australia

Van Nostrand Reinhold Company Limited
Molly Millars Lane
Wokingham, Berkshire, England

Library of Congress Cataloging in Publication Data

Wood, Margaret, 1950–
    Native American fashion.

    Bibliography: p.
    Includes index.
    1. Indians of North America—Costume and adornment.   I. Title.
E98.C8W66   746.9′2′08997   81-5012
ISBN 0-442-20756-5   AACR2

16 15 14 13 12 11 10 9 8 7 6 5 4 3 2 1

Contents

Introduction

Although there has recently been widespread interest in Native American arts and crafts, little attention has been paid to Native American decorative clothing. In this book I have surveyed the types of clothing worn by a number of different tribes and briefly explored the historical development of various clothing traditions. My intention has been to help establish contemporary adaptation of the rich, varied Native American clothing designs and styles. I hope too that this book will encourage young Native Americans to participate in and preserve the clothing heritage of our peoples. For this reason I have throughout the book included instructions on how to make some of the important garments.

It was also my desire to reveal the Native American woman as the talented designer, artist, and craftsperson she was and is. The historical photographs show breathtaking examples of clothing created under primitive conditions. Some are strikingly simple, others are extremely elaborate, but all are works of art.

Native American clothing design has not been a static art. The chapters that follow will show a constant evolution in Native American clothing that occurred before and continued after contact with the white man. My adaptations are a continuation of this process. For that reason and due to my personal preferences, I have tried to avoid faddism in my adaptations. For almost all of my adaptations I have chosen patterns that are what I judge to be classic contemporary dress styles. The final designs are ones which I trust will be durable.

Although I have made an effort to present clothing designs from tribes in all parts of the United States, I have made no effort to give equal time to different regions. I chose costumes on the basis of the ease with which they could be adapted for contemporary wear. Thus, although fringed antelope and deerskin dresses were the common attire of many tribes, you will find only a few conservative adaptations of such dresses in this book.

On the other hand, there is a heavy representation of Southwest tribal styles in the book. Southwest costumes are generally easier to adapt. The Southwestern tribes had early enough access to cotton and wool to give them several hundred years in which to develop their own use of textiles, yet, they were isolated enough from white civilization to permit uniquely Native American styles to develop. Generally, the clothing traditions of tribes in the other parts of the country were more rapidly engulfed by Anglo customs.

There is a second reason for my emphasis on Southwestern tribes. Almost all of the Native-American-style jewelry being purchased and worn today is produced by three Southwestern tribes—the Navajo, Zuni, and Hopi. The immense popularity of this jewelry has overtaken the country so rapidly that there are no set rules or guidelines about what clothing is appropriate to wear with the pieces. I have seen women wearing heavy squash blossom necklaces with V-neck evening gowns, or worse, with T-shirts. I have seen beautifully handcrafted bracelets worn with ruffled cuffs. I hope that the photographs in this book will illustrate suitable and attractive ways to wear Native-American-style jewelry.

In addition to the chapters on clothing of particular tribes and tribal groups, there is a final chapter on modern fabrics that make use of traditional Native American designs. In it, I present what is available and make suggestions for use of these fabrics in contemporary fashion.

A final word about the sewing instructions is needed. This is not a how-to-sew book; that information is available in other places. My instructions are general, not detailed, because I want to encourage creativity in the seamstress. Each person has their own individual tastes; so, wherever possible, I present a variety of design and accent features. I hope that seamstresses will follow the Native American practice of creating their own variations in design and garment construction, as defined by tribal custom. This is how Native American costume design has evolved in the past; I hope that this book will be a part of its continued evolution.

Map of the United States divided into tribal group areas.

1 Navajo Clothing Styles

 THE NAVAJO, celebrated weavers and silversmiths of the Southwest, are the nation's largest tribe of Native Americans. (See the map on page 7.) Today, more than 130,000 Navajo live on a reservation larger than the state of West Virginia, covering portions of three states—Arizona, New Mexico, and Utah. The versatile and ever-adapting Navajo have taken from neighboring tribes, the Spanish, and from other Europeans to form a unique culture and their own distinctive clothing styles.

Before the Spanish brought sheep to the Americas, the Navajo wove coarse garments from shredded bark or the fibers of the yucca cactus. Later, they used deer and antelope hides to produce clothing similar to, but less elaborate than, the clothing of the Plains tribes.

A seminomadic people, the Navajo were too dispersed and too warlike for the Spanish to colonize. Instead, the Spaniards brought their religion and flocks to the adobe villages of the neighboring Pueblo Indian tribes. It was in this indirect way that the Navajo became acquainted with wool. Through both raiding and trading with the Pueblos, the Navajo obtained sheep and a knowledge of weaving, and it was from these beginnings that a

1-1. *The old style* bil, *sometimes called the "blanket dress," was made from two handwoven oblong pieces fastened at the shoulders and along the sides and worn with a belt.* Courtesy Denver Art Museum, Denver Colorado.

1-2. *The clothing style shown here began to appear in the late 1860's. It is the Navajo version of the Victorian-style dress worn by Anglo women at that time.* Courtesy Denver Art Museum, Denver Colorado.

unique, truly Native American art form emerged—the Navajo blanket.

The Navajo *bil,* or "blanket dress," was the first distinctive Navajo contribution to Native American fashion. (See Figure 1-1.) As the name suggests, the dress was made from two oblong pieces, each handwoven like a Navajo blanket, fastened along the sides, and worn as a shift. The long sides were sewn from the bottom up, three-quarters of the length. The dress was worn using the open slits as armholes and was fastened at the shoulders with either stitches or pins of brass or silver.

Neither the variety of color nor the design found in modern Navajo rugs was used in the bil. The body of the dress was usually black or navy blue, an influence from the Pueblo weavers, with designs in red interwoven as trim at the shoulders and hem. There are a few known examples of blanket dresses done in gray with black trim. A Navajo lady of the 1800's wore a colorful sash belt, high-rising moccasins, and jewelry to complete her outfit.

In the late 1860's, after the Navajo returned from their captivity at Ft. Sumner, New Mexico, a new style began to evolve. It was during captivity that the Navajo came into daily contact with Anglo women for the first time. The Navajo women adapted the Victorian dresses into fitted blouses and full, gathered and tiered skirts. (See Figure 1-2.) Widespread use of the new style began shortly after the release of the Navajo in 1868.

After their return to the Navajo reservation, white traders appeared bringing bolts of brightly colored fabrics—cotton, corduroy, woolens, and, at the top of the line, velvet. Few trade items have ever been so enthusiastically received. The Navajo loved velvet for its richness, softness, and sheen. They also recognized, as do jewelers the world over, that velvet provides the ideal backdrop for jewelry. Most women made everyday blouses of cotton or corduroy and saved their velvet for dress-up occasions.

For more than a hundred years Navajo women have worn velvet and velveteen blouses with wide, tiered cotton skirts as their principal item of decorative clothing. Today, many older women still wear this outfit on an everyday basis, but younger women save their "traditional" clothes for special occasions. As the older people die, their clothes go with them. In its final stages, Navajo fashion has become costume. Its demise marks yet another step of assimilation—the end of the daily wear of these Native Americans.

1-3. *This adaptation of the* bil *uses the same colors and designs, but is floor length and more custom fitted.*

Often the Navajo blouse is accented with tucks and/or silver buttons. The origin of the use of tucks goes back to the days when scissors were unavailable. Fabric had to be ripped into appropriately sized pattern pieces. Tucks were used as a means of adding shape to the finished garment. Later, when patterns and scissors did become available, the tucks remained as decorations. Commonly, tucks are sewn on the sleeves in rows from the shoulder seam to the cuff, or simply sewn up from the cuff several inches and vertically on the front and the back of the blouse. When used, silver buttons sometimes follow the tucks, or, on other blouses, they may outline the blouse independently. For many years the Navajo prized silver coins, especially dimes, as decorative buttons. By soldering copper loops on one side, the Navajo easily transformed the coin into a fashion accessory. Silver buttons with stamped designs were also commonly used. Most frequently, the buttons were attached around the borders of the collar, down the front tab closure, across the yokes, around the cuffs, and set in rows down the sleeves. A wealthy Navajo woman of the 1870's would decorate her blouse with a hundred or more silver buttons. This custom predated the contemporary fashion industry's use of studs by more than a hundred years.

Navajo Blanket Dress Adaptation

The dress shown here is an adaptation of the Navajo blanket dress. The colors and design of the traditional dress were applied to a loosely fitted floor-length dress. The neckline and colors make this garment an excellent one on which to display jewelry, particularly older silver pieces. The design on the borders can be embroidered, appliqued, or a combination of the two.

PATTERN

Use any commercial pattern for a floor-length dress with a bateau neckline. A bateau neckline is cut in a shallow curve across the line of the collarbones almost to the tip of the shoulders. The cut is the same across the back of the neck. This neckline best simulates the line of the Navajo blanket dress.

The trim designs of the dress can be applied to any garment, but, because the colors are so strong and the pattern so bold, it is best to limit their use to larger garments, such as dresses, long skirts, and capes.

FABRIC

Use any medium- to heavyweight fabric. I made my dress from medium-weight wool. If working with knits, you will need to take care during the applique process to ensure that puckers and ripples do not form.

Stay with the color combinations the Navajo used—black or dark blue with red borders, or gray with black borders. If you deviate much from these, you will risk compromising the Native American flavor of the garment and its compatibility with jewelry.

The midriff section of a size 12 dress will require 1¼ yards (1.1 m) of 60-inch-wide (150-cm) fabric. The borders and applique pieces will require ⅞ yard (.8 m) of 60-inch-wide (150-cm) fabric.

SPECIAL INSTRUCTIONS

It is best to alter the dress pattern so that the top and bottom borders are separate pattern pieces. The top border of my dress is 10 inches (25.4 cm) wide, not including seam allowances, and the bottom border is 12 inches (30.4 cm) wide, not including seam allowances or hem. Alter both the front and the back dress pattern pieces. Use pattern-adjusting tissue paper to add seam allowances to border and midriff pattern pieces.

Lay out and cut out the pattern pieces you have created. Cut red fabric for the top and bottom borders and black or dark blue for the midriff section. For the gray/black color combination, cut black borders and a gray midriff section. Sew the borders to the midriff section.

Choose a border design motif from those given here or examine books on Navajo Indians and Navajo weaving. Enlarge the design elements so they appear proportional in size to the garment upon which they will be applied. Make paper patterns. If using an applique method, typing-weight paper is sufficient. If using an embroidery method, make pattern pieces out of posterboard or an equally heavy board.

Now is the time to check how your design motif selections actually look on the garment. Pin back dress pieces to the front dress piece, along the shoulder seams, and hang on a hanger or drape on a dress form. Use your paper design patterns and cut out design motif pieces from scrap fabric for sample design motifs. Pin the sample design motifs into position on the borders. Alter size or position as desired.

You can apply the designs on the borders using embroidery, applique, or a combination of the two, but it is best to apply large design elements by applique. Use your design motif paper pattern to cut design elements from black, dark blue, or gray wool. Also cut pieces of fusible web using the design motif pattern. The fusible web will prevent puckers that sometimes occur with applique work. It also helps stabilize the fabric against the stress of satin-stitching. Use the fusible web and your steam iron to position the design pieces on the borders and then use a machine satin stitch or close zigzag around the edges.

If you'd prefer to embroider your design, use crewel wool. Trace the design in the border using your paper pattern and fabric-marking chalk. The satin stitch will probably be the best overall stitch; but that depends on the size and type of design motif.

When you have completed decorating the borders, follow the printed dress pattern instructions to finish constructing the garment.

1-4. Authentic Navajo designs, which can be used as trim for the blanket dress.

1-5. *The fabric used for this Navajo-style shirt (left) will determine whether it is casual or dressy. The cotton knee-length skirt has been "broomstick pleated."*

Navajo-Style Skirt and Blouse

The adaptations pictured here are almost exact duplications of the long, gathered skirt and fitted blouse of the Navajo (see Figure 1-2), except, of course, for changes in the hem length and fullness of the skirt and for the sleeve length of the velveteen blouse.

The street-length skirt is tiered and gathered, but looks almost like an A-line skirt because it is "broomstick pleated." The origin of this special process is not documented, but it probably was the result of the Navajo women's need to control the wrinkles of the wide skirts in an area where irons were unavailable.

PATTERN

For a Navajo-style blouse, choose a commercial blouse pattern that is collared, open fronted (either with front placket closure or front neckline slit), and long sleeved, with or without cuffs, or with three-quarter-length sleeves.

Street or floor-length, tiered and gathered skirts are very popular today, and patterns are readily available in fabric stores; or, if you prefer, follow the steps under Special Instructions.

FABRIC

Use one-hundred percent cotton or a cotton blend for skirts that are to be broomstick pleated. Do not use permanent press fabric.

In addition to cotton, Navajo women sometimes use other fabrics for their skirts. Common fabric combinations for the blouse-skirt outfit are shown in the following chart.

Use a solid color or small-detailed prints for the skirt. Some Navajo women make both parts of the outfit in one color or tones of one color. Many wear white skirts with brightly colored blouses.

A size 12 Navajo-style blouse will require 2 yards (1.85 m) of 44/45-inch-wide (115-cm) fabric. The moderately full skirt with three tiers required 2¼ yards (2 m) of 44/45-inch-wide (115-cm) fabric. I used 1¼ widths of fabric in the top tier, 2½ widths in the middle tier, and 4 widths in the bottom tier. A long Navajo skirt will require from 3 to 5 yards (2.8 to 4.5 m) of 44/45-inch-wide (115-cm) fabric.

SPECIAL INSTRUCTIONS

Whether you are making a street- or floor-length skirt with two or three tiers, it can be constructed following these simple steps.

Two-Tiered Skirt

1. Measure a street- or floor-length skirt in your wardrobe to determine the desired finished length.

2. Divide the length in two for two tiers. This will give you an approximate length for each tier.

3. Add 1¼ inches (3.2 cm) for seam allowances to the top tier length measurement.

4. Add 2⅝ inches (6.7 cm) for one seam allowance and 2 inches (5 cm) for a hem to the bottom tier measurement.

5. Follow the cutting layout given here for a skirt that will hang well. It is important that the skirt, which will, of course, hang vertically, be cut across the vertical grainline of the fabric. This is especially important when using fabrics such as velvet or velveteen, which have naps that must run in the same direction.

6. Depending on the degree of fullness you desire, sew together 1½ to 2½ widths of fabric for the top tier and 2½ to 4 widths for the bottom tier. Of course, the width, in inches, of the fabric you've used will affect the number of widths you need.

Three-Tiered Skirt

1. Measure a street- or floor-length skirt in your wardrobe to determine the desired finished length.

2. Divide the length in three for three tiers. This will give you an approximate length for each tier.

3. Add 1¼ inches (3.2 cm) for seam allowances to the top and middle tier measurement.

4. Add 2⅝ inches (6.7 cm) for one seam allowance and 2 inches (5 cm) for the hem to the bottom tier measurement.

5. Cut the fabric into widths, as shown in Figure 1-6.

6. Most Navajo women sew together 2 to 2½ widths for the top tier, 3 to 5 widths for the middle tier, and 4½ to 6½ widths for the bottom tier.

Occasionally, you may see a floor-length skirt with only two tiers; more than three tiers are rarely used.

As you cut the skirt fabric, it is a good idea to stack widths in a separate pile for each tier. Cut a waistband of

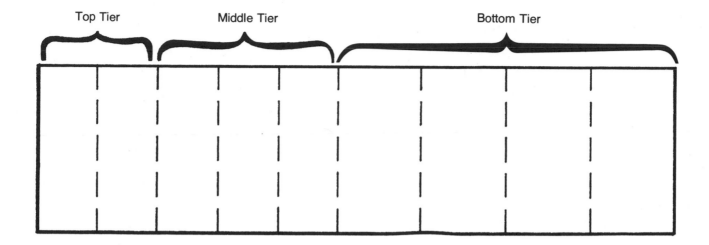

the fold-over type, from the same fabric, using the waist-band pattern piece from your favorite commercial skirt pattern.

Sew the widths for each tier together, side by side. Leave the long tier pieces flat; the remaining seam will be the center back seam. Stitch the upper edge of each tier inside the seam allowance with two rows of machine-basting. If you are making a two-tiered skirt, you need only gather the bottom tier to fit the lower edge of the top tier. If you are making a three-tiered skirt, gather the bottom tier evenly to the lower edge of the middle tier, then gather the top of the middle tier to fit the lower edge of the top tier.

For either two- or three-tier skirts, close the center back seam, installing a 7-inch (17.7-cm) zipper ⅝ of an inch (1.5 cm) below the top of the skirt. Gather the upper edge of the top tier to fit the waistband, following the printed pattern markings to allow for the waistband over-lap. Finish attaching the waistband according to the printed pattern instructions and hem the skirt.

Navajo women used to bunch the waistband of their skirts around a broomstick and tie the skirt tightly with string. An easier method, and the one you should use, ac-complishes the same result with a nylon stocking or with a length of pantyhose, the toe of which has been removed.

To broomstick pleat, the garment must be thor-oughly wet. Fold the waistband into 2-inch (5-cm) accor-dionlike folds, as shown. Holding the skirt by the folded waistband, pull downward all around the hem to make sure the fabric is perfectly aligned. Then pull the skirt, waistband first, through the stocking. Tie strings around the bunched-up skirt at the tier seams if the stocking does

1-6. Guide for cutting tiered skirt pattern pieces. After you have determined the length of your tiers, cut out the tier components across the fabric grainline. Each tier is fuller than the one above it. The bottom tier pieces look wider because they include a 2-inch (5-cm) hem allowance.

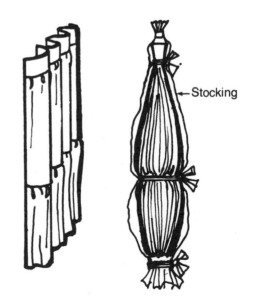

←Stocking

1-7. Broomstick pleating is a method of creating controlled wrinkles. Fold the skirt waistband accordion-style, stuff it into a nylon stocking, and tie string tightly at the tier seams.

1-8. *This outfit features the Navajo wedding basket design applique. The design is one of many distinctive Navajo motifs that can be applied to contemporary garments. A branch coral necklace sets the outfit off nicely.*

not seem to be holding the skirt tightly enough. It will take the skirt at least twenty-four hours to dry completely. It will dry with tight folds, but will not be permanently pleated. When not in use, store the skirt in a stocking, either hung from a hanger, or laid in a drawer. Packed this way, the skirt is excellent for travel.

At one time, most Navajo women applied rickrack as trim to the bottom of each tier. This is not done much anymore, probably because of the extensive use of satin and velvet skirt material. The satin is so shiny, it is thought perhaps that it doesn't need any more embellishment; furthermore, the nap of the velvet makes applying rickrack very difficult. If you do use cotton, for the skirt, however, you might add rickrack in a matching or contrasting color. Whatever the fabric, you might topstitch the tier seams in a matching color thread. Some Navajo women topstitch using a zigzag stitch.

Navajo Wedding Basket Pants Suit

Many traditional Navajo designs are suitable for transferring onto clothing. Here a Navajo design embellishes a pants suit.

This common and easy-to-work-with design is from the Navajo wedding basket, which is an important element in the Navajo wedding ceremony. It is a stair-step motif adapted from the shallow woven basket, usually 12 inches (30 cm) in diameter. The distinctive two-color design has been used by the Navajo in recent years on silver jewelry, purses, and beaded pieces. You can applique the decorative panel to just about any garment, even ready-made ones.

PATTERN

This stair-step design motif can be applied to almost any type of garment. Consider using it as trim down the front of a plain dress or skirt. If you want to create an outfit similar to the pants suit I made, select a commercial pants

21

pattern with straight or slightly flaired legs and a hip-length tunic top.

The pattern for the motif is given here. The size of your motif will vary with the type of garment.

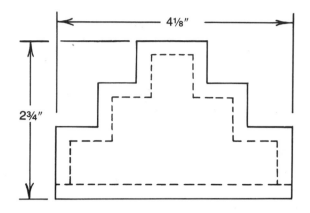

1-9. Pattern for Navajo Wedding Basket design.

FABRIC

Use a roughly woven polyester/cotton blend for the pants outfit and decorative panel. You might prefer to use a lightweight wool or other light- to medium-weight fabric. I do not recommend stretch or knit fabrics because the extensive applique work will pull them out of shape and cause puckers and ripples.

The pants suit I made is a natural color. Good color combinations for the motifs include black or dark brown stairs, with red, rust, or maroon center bands. I have also seen a very attractive example of this design with black stairs and a purple center.

A size 12 top will require 1½ yards (1.35 m) of 44/45-inch-wide (115-cm) fabric. Slacks will require 2½ yards (2.3 m) of 44/45-inch-wide (115-cm) fabric. The center band applique will require ⅛ yard (11.5 cm) and the stair-step applique pieces will require no more than ¼ yard (23 cm).

SPECIAL INSTRUCTIONS

Lay out and cut out the slacks and tunic top pattern pieces following the printed pattern instructions.

The best way to reproduce this design is to applique it. Figure 1-9 shows the basic design elements. If reproduced exactly, this pattern will produce a 5¾-inch-wide (15-cm) decorative panel, the size I used on the pants suit. You may want to enlarge or reduce the dimensions to produce a different effect on your garment.

After you have calculated the size of the pattern you

desire, cut the stair-step pattern piece from posterboard or other heavy paper. Use the paper pattern and, with a pencil, trace the outline of the design unit onto the fabric you have selected. If your sewing machine does a good zigzag or satin stitch, you can eliminate the turn-under allowance.

To apply the applique, first stitch the outside leg seams of the slacks and the side seams of the top. This way, you will have a flat surface on which to work, as you applique the motifs, and you can space evenly all around the garment.

To attach the motifs to the fabric, first lay out the design units on the garment. The bottom of the lower stair units on the tunic top are placed 1 inch (2.54 cm) above the finished length and those on the pants are 7 inches (18 cm) above the finished length. Evenly space the upside-down stair motifs. Calculate the width of the center band and where it will overlap. Space the upright stair motifs opposite the upside-down ones, allowing room for the band. Turn under all edges ¼ inch (6 mm) if you cannot use a machine zigzag or satin stitch. Press the hem and hand-baste the stair units in place. Use a regular sewing machine stitch to attach the stair motif units in place. If you will be using a zigzag or satin stitch, use your paper pattern to cut fusible web stair motifs. Use your steam iron to position and hold the stair units in place with the fusible web, which will prevent puckers and bulges that often occur in the applique piece. It also helps stabilize the fabric against the stress of satin stitching. Satin-stitch the edges of the stair-step motifs. It is unnecessary to stitch the bases of the stair motifs because they will be covered by the center band.

Cut the center band along the grain of your selected fabric. A pattern is unnecessary because it is a straight piece. Cut it to the width indicated in Figure 1-9 and a little longer than the pants leg or tunic top width. Fold the turn-under allowance of the band to the wrong side and press. Lay the band over the bases of the stair units, positioning it on the overlap lines, and hand-baste it in place. Use the straight topstitch on your sewing machine to attach it along both edges. It is not advisable to use a satin stitch for attaching the band because most machines cannot produce a good satin stitch on so many layers of fabric. Trim any extra band fabric.

Follow the printed pattern instructions to finish constructing the garments.

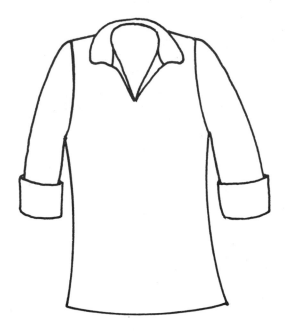

Navajo-Style Shirt

When Navajo women were still weaving their own dresses, they also wove fabrics for shirts and pants for the men. A man's shirt required four separately woven pieces—front and back pieces plus two sleeves. They were sewn together with yarn and were loose fitting so they could be easily pulled over the head. The practice of weaving this type of shirt was learned from the Pueblo Indian tribes whose men wore a similar shirt. (Figure 3-8 illustrates the basic concept of this simple shirt.)

As manufactured fabric became readily available, Navajo women made clothing from it. In time, many men and women accepted Anglo-style clothing for everyday wear. Just as most Navajo women save their velvet blouses and full skirts for special occasions, Navajo men wear their simply cut shirts usually with loose-fitting white pants for special occasions.

This plain shirt, very similar to the woman's top in Figure 1-5, is excellent for wearing with chokers, long necklaces, and pins. The "weight" of a heavy necklace is partially absorbed when worn under the collar. The shirt can be worn tucked in, loose, or belted.

PATTERN

The commercial pattern to use for a man's shirt is very similar to the one you would use for the woman's blouse (see Figure 1–5). It should have a collar, front-slit opening, and long or three-quarter length sleeves (with or without cuffs). Side slits are helpful because the garment is put on over the head.

FABRIC

Of course, the fabric you choose will largely determine the garment's suitability for casual or dressy wear. Since the shirt is usually worn for dress occasions, the Navajo, for the most part, make theirs of velvet, velveteen, or corduroy. If you want the shirt for everyday use, the fabric choice is optional. Navajo men usually wear deep purple, red, or navy blue, but again, the color is optional. Solid colors, rather than prints, are recommended.

A size 12 velveteen top will require about 2¾ yards (2.6 m) of 44/45-inch-wide (115-cm) fabric. Napped fabrics, such as velveteen, velvet, and corduroy, require more yardage than do fabrics without naps. For fabrics without naps, follow the yardage recommendations on the printed pattern.

SPECIAL INSTRUCTIONS

Follow the printed pattern instructions to construct the garment. Follow the Navajo example and wear this shirt over white pants. Both men and women look attractive in this outfit. Keep in mind too that the Indian flavor of the garment lies in the Indian jewelry you will wear with it.

2 Apache Clothing Styles

THE APACHE, at one time fierce warriors of the Southwest, are now scattered in relatively small groups or bands in Arizona, New Mexico, and Oklahoma. (See the map on page 7.)

Originally, the Apache wore skin garments, but changing life-styles and scarcity of game influenced their decision to accept manufactured cloth when it became available. One cause of these changing life-styles was the almost constant state of warfare with Anglos as they encroached more and more upon Apache lands. The war efforts often precluded hunting and, because the people were almost constantly on the move, the Apache were left with neither time nor place to tan hides. The Apache women probably adopted manufactured cloth because they had to.

The women of some of the Apache bands created a clothing style that consists of a full, gathered and tiered skirt and loose blouse. This is essentially a different interpretation of the Victorian dress, which inspired the Navajo women to create their full, gathered skirts and velvet blouses. (See page 11.)

Also known as a "camp dress" or a "Mother Hubbard," the skirt and blouse outfit is usually decorated with bands of trim around the yoke and the bottom of the skirt tiers. (See Figure 2-1.)

2-1. *The photograph shows a "camp dress," which has been worn by Apache women since the late 1800's. This was the Apache interpretation of the Victorian dress. The woman is holding a burden basket, which was used for gathering edible plants.* Courtesy Denver Art Museum, Denver, Colorado.

2-2. *This adaptation of the camp dress is made of yellow satin. The top is shorter and the skirt slimmer than those traditionally made by Apache women.*

Many older Apache women still wear the traditional camp dress every day. Some own both the older leather garments and the camp dress and wear them for tribal gatherings and festive occasions. Women of other desert tribes, such as the Papago, Yaqui, and Maricopa, also wear a similar two-piece garment.

Some Apache bands, such as the Jicarilla Apache in northernmost New Mexico, have never accepted this style of clothing. Located near the Great Plains, this band has for several centuries had much contact with Plains tribes. It now has more in common with them in terms of style of dress than it does with the other Apache bands.

Apache Camp Dress Adaptation

This is an adaptation of the traditional camp dress. The blouse of this adaptation is much shorter than are those made by Apache women. Since the Apache camp dress is rather heavily trimmed, you would want to wear only a few pieces of jewelry with it.

PATTERN

Choose a commercial pattern for a blouse that is yoked, front and back, gathered below the yokes, and collarless, with a short front-lapped opening. The sleeves can be short and puffed, long and cuffed, or three-quarter-length and cuffed.

The skirt is floor-length with two tiers (rarely three). Make it from a commercial pattern or follow the instructions for the Navajo skirts. (See page 17.) As a general rule, the Apache women make their skirts fuller than do most Navajo. Use the maximum number of fabric widths recommended for each tier.

Make the length of each tier equal or make the top tier two-thirds of the total length and the bottom tier one-third of the total length.

FABRIC

For the most part, Apache women make these skirts out of cotton, usually in a small floral print, with a trim of a matching color. Not as popular but still used are solid colors of cotton. Many women make the outfit with a print fabric and black trim probably because it contrasts so well. Some use two or three colors of trim selected to match the colors of a print fabric.

In recent times, since the young women reserve their "traditional" wear for special occasions, other fabrics, such as velvet, lined chiffonlike fabric, voile, and satin, are substituted. Whenever possible, prints are used, but the velvet and satin fabrics are in bright, solid colors.

Trim bands are rarely wider than ⅜ inch (9 mm). They may be made of rickrack, bias tape, middy braid, thin ribbon, or strips of cloth. One row of stitching is usually enough to secure a band.

A size 12 Apache-style top requires 2 yards (1.85 m) of 44/45-inch-wide (115-cm) fabric. A skirt of this fullness will require about 2½ yards (2.3 m) of fabric. I used 14½ yards (13 m) of black middy braid to decorate the outfit.

SPECIAL INSTRUCTIONS

Use your printed pattern instructions to lay out and cut the fabric for the blouse. It is wise to attach the trim before constructing the garment completely. To attach the trim to the yoke, join front and back yoke pieces at the shoulder seams and sew on the trim. Then sew together the rest of the pieces following the printed pattern instructions. If you will be adding trim to the cuffs, it is best to do so before you attach them to the sleeves. It is easier to attach the trim to the skirt tiers while they are still ungathered and unassembled.

Many examples of Apache camp dresses have one, two, or three bands of trim around the yoke (and sometimes on sleeve cuffs) and the same number around the bottom of each skirt tier. In recent years the trim has become lavish. Examination of recently made garments and photographs of contemporary garments show that trim on skirts is indeed becoming very heavy. I recently saw two skirts that sported eighteen and twenty-four bands of trim around the skirt. (Figure 2-3 shows the placement of the bands on these outfits.)

2-3. *Trim on two contemporary Apache outfits.*

3 Pueblo Clothing Styles

 WHEN THE SPANISH entered the Southwest in 1540, some Native Americans were already living in compact, many-chambered, flat-roofed structures built around central squares. The Spaniards, reminded of the villages back home, called these settlements *pueblos*, the Spanish word for village, and thus, the village dwellers became known as Pueblo Indians.

The Pueblo Indians are decendants of a tribal people known as the "Basket Makers." These people first grouped into an identifiable culture prior to the fourth century A. D. and inhabited the Four Corners region—the area where the corners of Arizona, New Mexico, Colorado, and Utah touch. (See the map on page 7.) As climate changed, the Basket Makers began to migrate to the Rio Grande River Valley, which is in present-day New Mexico, and settled into villages.

Prior to and during the early development of the Basket Maker culture, simple leather garments were worn by the tribespeople. By the twelfth century A. D., they were cultivating cotton for the purpose of weaving and using looms to weave dresses, shawls, blankets, shirts, kilts, and other articles of clothing. Among Pueblo tribespeople, it is commonly the men who do the weaving. Cotton was

used in pre-Spanish times, and wool thereafter, although some ceremonial garments have always been woven of cotton.

After the Basket Maker people began weaving cloth, it is believed that the first upper body woven coverings were little more than a rectangular piece worn like a poncho with a hole for the head. Later the sides were closed and sleeves added. Before the sides were sewn, the sleeves were attached adjacent to the neck opening and slightly overlapping the shoulder edge. A simple running stitch was used to attach it to the main part of the top, and then the sides were closed. Slits left at the bottom of the side seams were common.

Cotton shirts were in natural colors or were dyed. Most wool shirts were dyed navy blue, black, or dark brown. Some of the shirts were plain, while embroidery adorned others. (Figure 3-1 illustrates the shirt in heavily embroidered cotton.)

The common dress for all Pueblo women, the *manta*, has been worn for about four hundred years. (See Figure 3-2.) Named for the Spanish word for a square piece of fabric, it consists of a rectangle of dark brown, black, or blue handwoven cloth. It usually consists of three lengths sewn together to make a single piece wide enough to reach from the shoulder to the middle of the calf. A 20-inch-

3-1. *This Jemez Pueblo shirt is of cotton embroidered with red and black wool yarn.* Courtesy of Denver Art Museum, Denver, Colorado.

3-2. *This photograph taken in 1898 shows the* manta *as it was worn by Pueblo women for centuries.* Courtesy Smithsonian Institution National Anthropological Archives. Photo. No. 32,357-B.

wide (51-cm) twill-weave middle strip is bordered by 7-inch-wide (18-cm) bands at top and bottom. Common color combinations for the center band are black with dark blue borders or brown with black borders. With the introduction of manufactured cloth by Europeans, some Pueblo women began wearing mantas of wool, as well as calico and striped cottons.

The Pueblo women wrap the piece under the left arm and over the right shoulder. Then the garment may be pinned on or sewn at the shoulder and right side. The means of closing varies from village to village. Most Pueblo women use green and red yarn to close the right side and to trim along neck and hem edges.

In ancient times, the manta alone comprised the women's costume. Upon contact with Anglos and the introduction of manufactured cotton cloth, the underdress became a part of their standard way of dress. The underdress is a high-collared, long-sleeved dress that is worn under the manta. Some sources say the Pueblo women welcomed the cotton and used the underdress as sort of a soft lining to protect their skins from the rough, hand-woven wool of the manta. Other sources indicate that the underdress idea was more or less forced upon the Pueblo women by puritanical Anglos who were offended by the exposure of the bare shoulder and arms. Nonetheless, in the late nineteenth and early twentieth centuries, when the underdress was common, Pueblo women did not wear it during ceremonial and religious rites and dances. Even today, in certain religious ceremonies, the underdress is not worn.

Some older Pueblo women wear the manta every day, while young women save theirs for tribal gatherings and ceremonies. On the other hand, in most Pueblo ceremonials, men, or at least the dancers, wear a woven kilt. (See Figures 3-3 and 3-4.) Characteristically, this kilt is of white cotton with a woven-in design. The design, in red, green, and black, always follows a basic pattern and it symbolizes rain, clouds, growing crops, and life in general. The stairlike portions represent rain clouds, the vertical lines are the rain, and the horizontal green stripe represents the crops. A black band about 1 inch (2.5 cm) wide is usually embroidered around the bottom of the kilt. At intervals, 2- by 1-inch (4.8- by 2.5-cm) oblongs extend from the band into the white of the kilt. It is believed that in prehistoric and early historic times, this garment was worn by men every day, weather permitting, and that it was only later that it became a ceremonial garment.

3-3. *The woven kilt worn by a Pueblo man.* Courtesy Smithsonian Institution National Anthropological Archives. Photo. No. 1810.

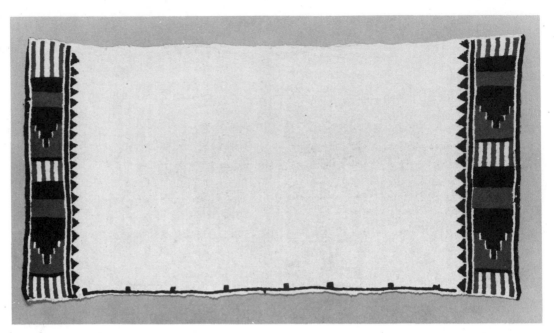

3-4. The kilts are of white cotton with a woven design in red, green, and black. Courtesy Denver Art Museum, Denver, Colorado.

In recent years, the design has been used on men's shirts and a few weavers are weaving this design for purses, shawls, and other garments for sale to the public.

Pueblo Manta-Style Top

I have converted the traditional manta into a top that can be worn with either slacks or a skirt. You may want to make both the accompanying slacks and skirt—the slacks make the outfit suitable for more informal wear, while a long skirt makes it dressier. Either way, the outfit looks particularly beautiful when worn with silver necklaces, bracelets, earrings, concho belts, and Pueblo woven sash belts.

PATTERN

Commercial patterns for one-shouldered garments are available, but you may have to reverse the pattern so that the left shoulder is bare. You might also convert the manta attractively into a long dress with an A-line or slim skirt.

3-5. *The outfit shown is an adaptation of the manta. The top is adorned with sewn-on strands of red and green yarn.*

The pattern will probably include an underarm zipper opening under the left arm.

FABRIC

Most mantas currently made are in solid black, although some are still produced in the three strips. To simplify things, I recommend using black fabric, as it helps identify the manta as Pueblo influenced. A very dark blue or brown would be authentic also, but might clash with the red and green trim to be used around the neck, hem, and right side. White fabric with the two-color trim would be easily recognizable as Pueblo influenced, since some ceremonial mantas are woven of white cotton.

Regardless of color, I recommend wool and heavy knits. Velvet or velveteen would also make lovely garments of this style.

A size 12 manta top will require 1 yard (.9 m) of 60-inch-wide (150-cm) fabric. A slim skirt will require 1⅜ yards (1.2 m) of fabric.

The green and red yarn trim, attached with an overcast-type stitch in regular sewing thread, gives the garment a Pueblo look. You can attach very thick yarn, or you might embroider the trim with crewel yarn. Occasionally, some Pueblo women use red or green alone.

SPECIAL INSTRUCTIONS

Follow the printed pattern instructions to construct the garment. As mentioned before, you might have to use the reverse side of the pattern pieces so that the left shoulder is the one that is bare. Complete the garment before attaching the trim.

Attach the trim 1½ inches (3.8 cm) from the "neckline"; that is, starting at the left underarm zipper, up over the right shoulder, and across the back to the left underarm again. Also, unless you have made a dress rather than a top, attach it the same distance above the finished bottom hem. You may want to follow what some Pueblo women do and leave 2 to 3 inches (5 to 7.5 cm) of yarn free at side seams and knot them to form small tassels. If you use both colors of trim, it does not matter whether you apply red above green or green above red when you attach the trim. Do not decorate the slacks or skirt.

If you have made a dress, you will want to apply the upper trim as you did on the top garment, but you should apply the lower trim about 4 inches (10 cm) above the finished hem.

Pueblo-Style Skirt

Among several Pueblo tribes, especially the Zuni, it is customary for the manta to be closed with large turquoise and silver pins from the waist down. This type of manta closing is reserved for special occasions rather than everyday wear. Shown here is my adaptation of this fashion idea.

PATTERN

For this adaptation, use a basic wraparound commercial skirt pattern, with or without waistband. Length is optional. However, fashion today rules that the skirt be closed down your left side. It is your choice whether to follow the rule or reverse the pattern so that the Pueblo tradition of closing on the right side is followed.

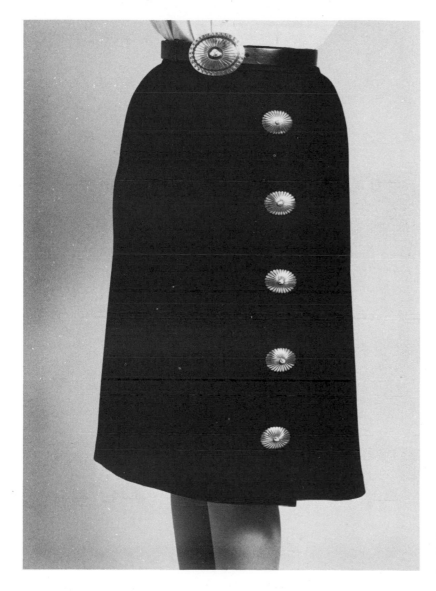

3-6. *This black wool skirt, also an adaptation of the manta, is decorated with six silver and turquoise belt conchos.*

39

3-7. *The wraparound skirt, decorated with the Pueblo kilt design. Hopi silver overlay jewelry complements it.*

FABRIC

I made this skirt in black wool because it is the color most commonly used in mantas and because black serves as an excellent background for the silver and turquoise. However, you can use any color. It is best to make the skirt with medium- to heavyweight fabric because the weight of the pins, buttons, or conchos will pull a delicate or lightweight fabric out of shape.

This street–length wraparound skirt in size 12 will require about 1⅝ yards (1.4 m) of 60-inch-wide (150-cm) fabric.

SPECIAL INSTRUCTIONS

Follow the pattern directions and complete the skirt before starting the decoration. In this version, I used large matching silver and turquoise conchos from a concho belt, instead of pins. (A concho belt is a belt made up of six to twelve conchos, or silver medallions, with or without stone settings. The number of conchos is determined by their size and the wearer's waist measurement. The conchos are usually strung on a leather strip by means of copper loops attached to the back of each concho. Usually, they can be easily removed and the loop can be used as a means of sewing them on garments.) I added large snaps to close the skirt because the shape of the conchos would have made buttonholing difficult. If you have five or six silver and turquoise pins of similar size and style, use them to close the skirt; or, you might use silver buttons, instead.

Pueblo Kilt Adaptation

My adaptation of the kilt is an attractive long skirt. I applied designs with a simple fabric dyeing process (liquid embroidery) accented with black grosgrain ribbon.

PATTERN

For this adaptation, use a commercial wraparound skirt pattern with a waistband. Length is optional. Keep in mind, too, that the design can be applied to almost any type of garment.

FABRIC

I do not recommend that you change the colors of the design. The red, green, and black design shows up nicely against the traditional white of the garment. if you do want to try something other than white for the garment, choose a color that does not clash with the colors of the design.

The fabric I used here is handwoven cotton, similar to the traditional garment, although wool or some other medium-weight fabric would be suitable.

A size 12 floor-length wraparound skirt will require 2½ yards (2.3 m) of 44/45-inch- (115-cm) or 60-inch-wide (150-cm) fabric. In addition, I used 1⅝ yards (1.5 m) of ⅜-inch-wide (9-mm) black ribbon to complete the horizontal lines of the design. I used 2⅜ yards (2.2 m) of ⅞-inch-wide (2.1-cm) black ribbon to border the decorative strip and 3½ yards (3.2 m) of ⅞-inch-wide (2.1-cm) black ribbon to trim the bottom of the skirt.

SPECIAL INSTRUCTIONS

Cut out the garment pieces following the commercial pattern instructions. Apply the Pueblo design to the appropriate unassembled garment piece or to a separate strip of fabric.

You can apply the design to the garment in a number of different ways, including applique or embroidery. The method I used is a combination of liquid embroidery and ribbon applique. (Liquid embroidery is a method of painting color on fabric using what looks like a giant ball-point pen head and tubes of ink especially designed for use on fabric. Liquid embroidery supplies and instructions are available at hobby and craft stores.)

Rather than applying the design directly to the front of the skirt, you may want to do as I did and apply the design to a separate piece of the same fabric and then attach the decorated cloth strip to the skirt front. This way, you have less fabric to struggle with while applying the design and also less loss of materials in case you make a mistake.

To produce the decorative strip, first determine the appropriate size of design for your needs. You can adjust the size of the design so that the whole decorative strip is in proportion to the garment. On my skirt, each complete design unit (see Figure 3-8) is 7 inches (18 cm) tall. The unit is 5¼ inches (13 cm) wide, not including black trim on either side. You may want to calculate design unit size so that the completed decorative strip consists of whole design units. This is not absolutely necessary though, because there are enough horizontal lines in each unit to accommodate breaking off a design unit where needed.

There are no set rules as to the arrangement of the components of the decorative unit. For instance, I have seen designs where the stairstep portion was upright, upside down, and, in one instance, where two were stacked with the narrow ends almost touching. If you want some variety in the design, check Pueblo Indian books, paintings, and artifacts.

Once you decide on size, draw an enlarged design unit on paper. Trace and make a posterboard pattern for the stair portion of the design unit. The rest of the design can be easily transferred and applied with a ruler. Use a lead or fabric-marking pencil to transfer the measurements from the design you have drawn onto the garment. Mark the straight lines of the design with the ruler. Position and trace around the stair pattern. Trace design units one under another until the decorative strip is completed.

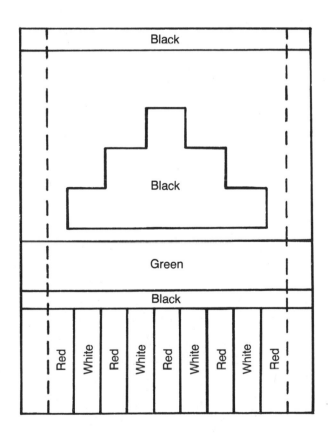

3-8. *Pattern for Pueblo kilt design.*   43

Use black liquid embroidery for the stair unit only. It is best to use black ribbon for the remaining black horizontal lines and edge trim. Fill in the green horizontal lines and red vertical lines with liquid embroidery. Alternate the red with unmarked white fabric stripes. Sew on ⅜-inch (8-mm) black grosgrain ribbon for the horizontal lines to complete the design units. If you have used a cloth strip for the decorative work, hand-baste it to the skirt front parallel to the grain of the fabric.

Whether you have basted on the decorated cloth strip or applied the Pueblo design directly to the garment piece, sew ⅞-inch-wide (2.1-cm) black grosgrain ribbon along both sides, overlapping the edges about ¼ inch (6 mm).

Follow printed pattern instructions to complete the garment.

To finish the bottom of the skirt in an authentic way first determine the finished length of the skirt plus ¼ inch (6 mm) and cut off any excess. Turn ¼ inch (6 mm) to the right side and press. The short vertical lines are ⅞-inch-wide (2.1-cm) grosgrain ribbon cut into 2¾-inch (7-cm) lengths. Place two short vertical pieces ½ inch (1.2 cm) apart and 5 inches (13 cm) from the next set of two. Place the edge of the short pieces ½ inch (1.2 cm) above the bottom of the skirt. Stitch each in place, turning under ¼ inch (6 mm) on the top. After all the vertical pieces are in place, stitch a long piece of grosgrain ribbon all around the bottom edge, extending it over the bottom of the skirt edge slightly. Stitch both edges of the ribbon.

Pueblo-Style Shirt and Slacks Outfit

This outfit is an adaptation of the Pueblo men's shirt shown in Figure 3-1. The plain neckline of the top is excellent for displaying jewelry of all types. It can be worn with slacks as it is here, or skirts, or it can be adapted as a dress. Thin ribbons are sewn on the garments to reproduce traditional decorative techniques.

3-9. *In this shirt and slacks outfit handwoven Mexican cotton simulates the handwoven Pueblo cotton from which the genuine article would be made. The black decorations are sewn-on ribbons.*

PATTERN

Choose a commercial pattern for a collarless, V-neck or front-slit-opening shirt, with long, cuffless sleeves. For a top that slips over the head, side slits are helpful and authentic. For a more fitted top, use a pattern with back darts and a zipper. Choose a pattern for accompanying slacks (or skirt, if you prefer).

FABRIC

A rough-woven white cotton fabric is authentic, but white or cream-colored wool would also be suitable. If you prefer darker colors, such as dark blue, black, or dark brown, I suggest wool.

A size 12 top requires 1¾ yards (1.6 m) of 44/45-inch-wide (115-cm) fabric. Slacks will require about 2½ yards (2.3 m) of fabric. I used 3¾ yards (3.5 m) of ⅜-inch-wide (9-mm) black ribbon to decorate the top and 1⅛ yards (1 m) of ⅞-inch-wide (2.1-cm) ribbon to decorate the bottom of the pants legs.

SPECIAL INSTRUCTIONS

Cut out the garment pieces following the commercial pattern instructions. It will be easier to decorate the garment pieces before they are assembled.

For the decoration I used black ⅜-inch (1-cm) grosgrain ribbon. Red alone or in combination with black on a white garment would also be attractive and authentic. Should you decide to do very simple designs on the shirt (see the upper right hand corner of Figure 3-10), use ⅞-inch-wide (2.1-cm) ribbon. If you are using a dark color fabric, decorate with red ribbon. Follow the sample design layouts or examine books on Pueblo Indians for additional design ideas.

Hand-baste the ribbon in position, folding the ribbon as needed at corners, and turn under ends ¼ inch (6 mm). Machine-stitch on all edges.

To simulate the old way of attaching the sleeves to the garment, you might want to topstitch on the garment near the shoulder seams with bottonhole twist or sew a simple running stitch with embroidery floss. Use red or black thread so it will be visible. Follow printed pattern instructions to complete the garment.

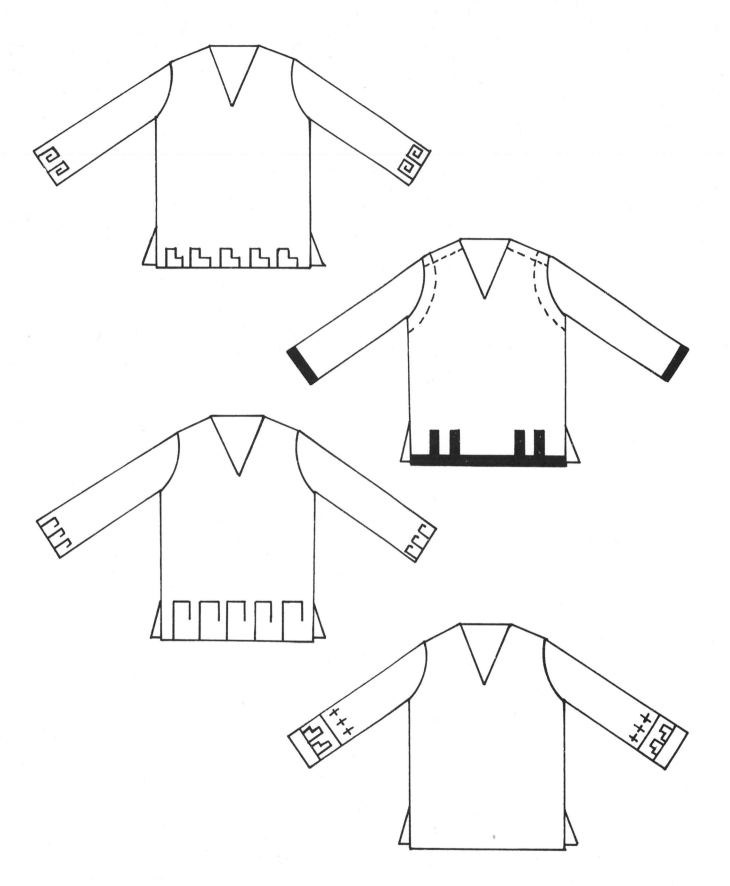

3-10. *Designs for the Pueblo-style shirt.*

4 Seminole Clothing Styles

 DESCENDANTS OF THE TRIBES of the Creek Confederacy, the Seminoles, whose name means "wild, untamed," moved from Georgia to Florida in the mid-eighteenth century to escape encroachment by white settlers. (See the map on page 7.) Contact between Anglos and the Florida Seminoles began again in the 1800's.

Some of the earliest known clothes worn by the Seminoles consisted of wraparound skirts woven of Spanish moss. Later, the Seminoles made clothing from tanned hides and, once it became available, from manufactured cloth, particularly cotton.

The Seminoles have evolved their own unique fashion—clothing adorned with vivid geometric patchwork designs. It is a unique method of constructing patchwork bands; what appears very complex at first is actually a simple well-planned process. (See Figures 4–1 and 4–2.)

There are numerous theories about the origin of Seminole patchwork. It is known that simple patchwork appeared in the late 1830's, during and after the Seminole Wars. The Seminole Wars were the result of the United States government's efforts to remove the Florida Seminoles to Indian Territory (present-day Oklahoma). Some Seminole people surrendered or were captured and sent

4–1. *This woman's costume shows the very beginnings of Seminole patchwork. The piecework consists mainly of bands of fabric. The top is still a blouse with a large collar.* Courtesy Denver Art Museum, Denver Colorado.

4-2. *In this photograph the last steps in the evolution of Seminole fashion can be seen. The women wear dozens of strands of beads which completely conceal their necks. The tops have become capes. Notice how the skirts sweep the ground. Seminole men who previously wore dresslike garments have exchanged pants for the full skirt. The dresslike garments have shortened into full shirts.* Courtesy Smithsonian Institution of Anthropological Archives, Bureau of American Ethnology Collection. Photo. No. 1178-M-2-C.

west. Others fought and retreated into swamp land where the United States military was at a disadvantage. Seminole reservations in Florida today consist of the same swamp land. The few hundred Seminoles who fled into the swamps in the 1830's and 1840's have increased to several thousand.

It was during the Seminole War era that the first simple patchwork garments appeared. One explanation for their development is that the war left Indian women so impoverished that they had to sew rags together (like crazy quilts) for clothing. Another source suggests that the technique evolved because cotton fabric was such a luxury. The patchwork technique was developed as a thrifty way to make use of even the tiniest scrap of fabric.

The first clothes made in the patchwork technique were interpretations of clothing worn by white men. In the late 1700's, some tribesmen began to wear a garment that was apparently derived from both the European tail-coat and the military uniform. With the wraparound, knee-length, coatlike garment, the men wore a turban, which was often embellished with ostrich feathers. The outfit included a white shirt and a wide belt; also, a silver crescent-shaped gorget, or disc, which was adopted from the fifteenth-century military men in Europe, was worn as a necklace. Moccasins completed the outfit. (See Figure 4-3.)

(The Seminoles were not alone in their imitation of the military coat. Variations of such were found among the Creek, Cherokee, Iroquois, Shawnee, Muskogee,

4-3. *This old drawing shows the Seminole leader, Tuko-see-mathla, wearing the military coat adaptation common to many Eastern and Southeastern tribes.* Courtesy Smithsonian Office of Anthropology. Photo. No. 45,112-F.

Winnebago, Chippewa, and others. While most widely worn by tribes in the Southeast, the coat was worn all along the East Coast and in the Great Lakes area. The military coat was one of the first European fashions to strongly influence Native Americans.)

The first of the coatlike garments were made of solid color, striped, or calico cotton. Later, the Seminoles kept the basic cut of the garment, but began enhancing the fabric from which it was sewn.

At first, Seminole women added bands of contrasting fabric to the cuffs and hems of the men's coats and to their own skirts. Later, the bands gave way to simple patchwork bands and then to more complicated patchwork. In garments that can be dated, there is a steady progression from solid color horizontal bands to more complicated geometric patchwork. The older garments are trimmed with one or a few patchwork bands, while some modern pieces are composed almost entirely of patchwork bands. (See Figures 4–1 and 4–2.)

The influence of the English and Frenchman's shirt of the time is reflected in some examples of the military coat adaptation. The Seminole transferred the ruffles on the European shirt to edge the collar and enhance the shoulder seam and the cuffs of the coat. The full sleeves were gathered at both wrists and shoulder, and this feature survives in contemporary Seminole men's jackets.

In the evolution from the military-coat style to the contemporary Seminole man's jacket, not only did the fabric change drastically, but so did the pattern. The top became fuller and front and back yokes were added. The full blouse was gathered into a waistband to which a gathered skirt was attached. The skirts were knee- or calf-length.

In recent times, Seminole men have adopted modern dress. One remnant of the old-style clothing is a shirt/jacket with a waistband. It is made of horizontal patchwork bands, usually with black as the background color. It is basically the long garment with the skirt left off.

The introduction of treadle sewing machines in the early twentieth century made small, more detailed designs possible, but there is some discrepancy concerning *when* the intricate designs seen today actually began to appear. According to one source, they came into being in the 1800's, but another source just as strongly states that the elaborate patchwork costumes did not appear until the 1920's.

If anything, this art form is still evolving. Seminole women and a few women from related tribes are still designing and devising new patterns of patchwork.

The late-nineteenth century costume of Seminole women consisted of a gathered floor-length skirt made of horizontal bands of simple cotton patchwork strips. Between patchwork bands solid-colored strips were sewn. The patchwork bands were edged with narrow appliqued bands of fabric, and a full-sleeved blouse with a large, flounced collar was worn with the skirt.

In recent times, the large collar has grown; the woman's upper garment is now a capelike affair. Gathered material is sewn to a narrow neck yoke. The cape is about wrist length. The bottom of the cape is decorated with bands of colorful applique, a single band of patchwork and lace, or a combination of two or all three. Photographs show some old patchwork skirts and capes made of small-detailed print cotton, but recent garments are made of solid-color fabrics for patchwork with the cape made of chiffon. Very few seminole women still wear this outfit for everyday purposes. Usually, they reserve it for festivals and special occasions. Many of the contemporary garments are made of satin or other shiny fabrics.

Before you attempt to create a Seminole patchwork garment, it is a good idea to study the technique. Figures 4–4 through 4–17 should help you. In the drawings, each patterned section denotes a color. Widths of pieces within patchwork bands are roughly in proportion.

Make some practice patchwork bands in scrap fabric before working with your good fabric. The practice will help you work out a system of assembly and will also help you determine how wide to make your cloth strips.

When making patchwork, seam allowances should be ¼ inch (6 mm) wide. The narrowest strips you can easily handle are ¾ inch (2 cm) wide, and, since ½ inch (1.2 cm) of this is for seam allowances, that leaves ¼ inch (6 mm) showing in the patchwork. An excellent cutting guide is a yardstick taped onto a gridded cardboard cutting board. Line the fabric to a grid line and use the yardstick to guide the scissors. Frequently press seams open or press them all in one direction. When you are calculating widths for fabric strips that make up the patchwork, be sure to allow extra fabric for both the top and the bottom strips in order to compensate for the seam allowances in addition to the waste that is created as a result of the off-set step.

Sample Seminole Patchwork Patterns

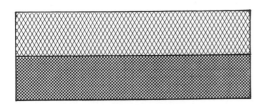

4-4. *Sew together strips of equal width. Press the seams open.*

Here are five different patchwork designs for you to try.

PATCHWORK PATTERN #1

This is a good design to practice first, as it is the simplest. At the same time, it entails all of the basic steps of making patchwork, so, once you have completed a length of this pattern, you will know what Seminole patchwork is all about. The technique for this patern can be used with any number of colors. Seminole women often use three to six shades of one color and arrange them in order from lightest to darkest. (See Figures 4-4 through 4-7.)

PATCHWORK PATTERN #2

This is done in very much the same technique as Pattern #1. It only looks like more work. (See Figures 4-8 and 4-9.)

PATCHWORK PATTERN #3

This pattern adds to the basic technique one of the many small tricks Seminole women have discovered to make the patchwork patterns look so very different from one another. Using the colors suggested, you will create a "Lazy T" design. You can change the look significantly if you use the color of the narrow, inner strips for the narrow band sewn to the side. This change will produce a ladder-like design. (See Figures 4-10 through 4-12.)

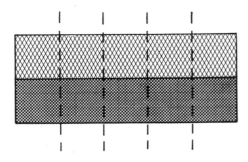

4-5. *Cut the strip into small, equal-sized segments, as indicated by the dashed lines.*

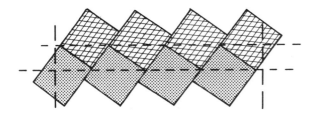

4-6. *Position each segment so that it is offset from the next, and sew them together, as shown. Trim the jagged edges and square off the ends, as indicated by the dashed lines. A sawtooth design remains.*

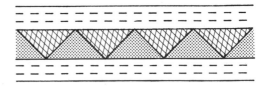

4-7. *One method of finishing the raw edges of a patchwork strip is to overlap them with bias tape, as shown.*

54

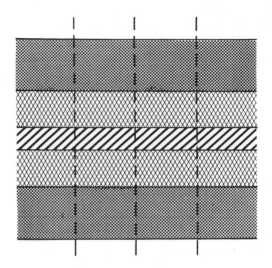

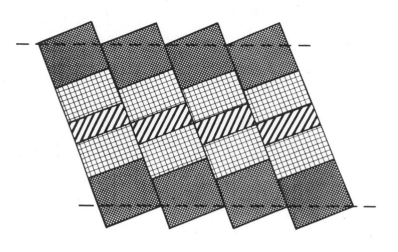

4-8. *Sew bias tape down the center of a wide band of another color. Sew strips of a third color on each side of the wide band. Cut the assembled strip into segments, as shown by the dashed lines.*

4-9. *Position the segments, as shown. Sew the sections together, matching the corners of the bias tape. Trim the points and square off the ends.*

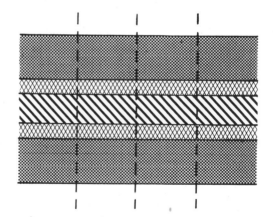

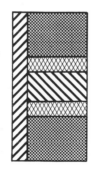

4-10. *Sew two narrow bands of one color to each side of a wider band of a second color. Then sew two wide bands of a third color to each side of the narrow bands. Press the seams open. Cut into small segments, as indicated by the dashed lines.*

4-11. *Sew narrow strips of cloth to one side of each small segment. Here, the side band is of the same fabric as the center band. For a completely different look, use the color of the two inner bands for the side band.*

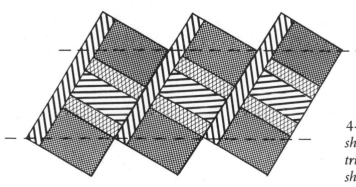

4-12. *Matching the two narrow inner bands as shown, sew the segments together. Press the seams, trim the jagged edges, and square off the ends, as shown.*

55

PATCHWORK PATTERN #4

The trick here is cutting the segments on an angle. Many different color combinations are possible. It is particularly interesting when you use two narrow bands of cloth in the center instead of just one. (See Figures 4-13 and 4-14.)

PATCHWORK PATTERN #5

This can be done in either two or three colors. It is depicted as two colors in the illustrations. If you want to use three colors, however, make one wide and one narrow strip on one color and the other wide and narrow strips two different colors. (See Figures 4-15 through 4-17.)

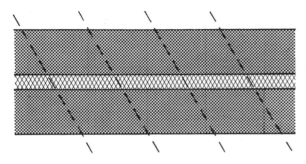

4-13. *Sew wide strips of cloth to either side of narrow strip of cloth in a second color. Cut the strip into segments on the diagonal, as shown by the dashed lines. A sixty-degree angle was used in the example.*

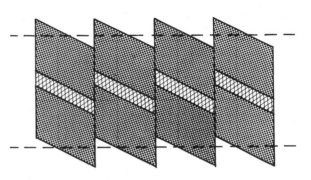

4-14. *Position the segments, as shown, and sew them together. Trim the points. The ends are already square.*

4-15. *Sew together a wide and a narrow strip each of two different colors, as shown. Cut segments along the dashed lines. These segments should be fairly narrow.*

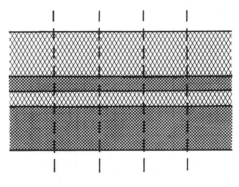

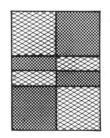

4-16. *Reverse alternate segments and sew pairs of segments together.*

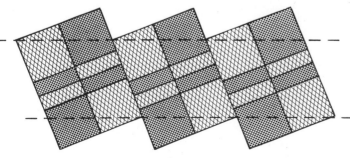

4-17. *Position the paired segments in an offset manner, and sew together. Trim the points along the dotted lines and square off the ends.*

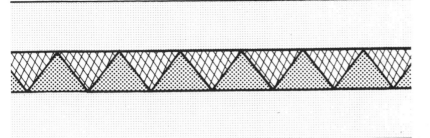

4-18. *Sew wide strips of a background color fabric to either side of your patchwork strip. A skirt or jacket will require up to six patchwork strips joined by background color strips to make enough yardage to cut out need pattern pieces.*

FINISHING THE PATCHWORK BANDS

The completed patchwork bands will vary in width depending on the patchwork designs you use and the widths of the cloth strips. For ideas and instructions on how to make other patchwork designs, check books and magazine articles on Seminole patchwork. (*Strip Patchwork* by Taimi Dudley, published by Van Nostrand Reinhold, is a good source for ideas.)

Once you have completed the patchwork bands, there are several ways to finish the edges and incorporate them into a garment. If you want to apply one band of patchwork to a garment, the bias tape method (illustrated in Figure 4-7) is the best. First, position the band on the fabric to which it is to be attached, lay bias tape over the edges of the patchwork. Then sew through the tape, the patchwork, and also the fabric to which the band is being attached.

If you are making a project that consists almost entirely of patchwork bands, you will want to do as the Seminole women do and connect the bands with fabric strips which are of one color and are of a width roughly equal to the average widths of the patchwork bands. (See Figure 4-18.) Sometimes Seminole women add thin bands of cloth applique and rickrack near the patchwork band, which make the band look wider and more intricate. (See Figure 4-19.) The thin bands of trim are not more than ⅜ inch (9 mm) wide. To make applique trim, cut strips of cloth ¾ to 1⅛ inch (1.8 to 2.8 cm) wide. Fold and press into thirds, lengthwise. Sew into position with the raw edges down, using one or two rows of machine-stitching. The rickrack is of the smallest available, sometimes called "baby rickrack."

Some Seminole seamstresses sew thin strips of cloth to each side of the patchwork band before sewing the widened band to the background strip. (See Figure 4-20.)

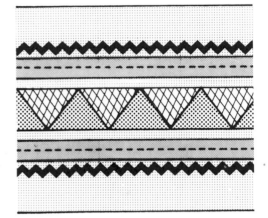

4-19. *Enhance the patchwork strips by adding many rows of rickrack and thin cloth applique. This helps make the patchwork strip look wider.*

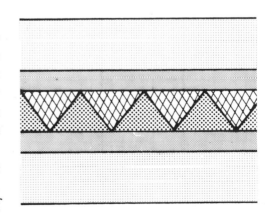

4-20. *Another way to make the patchwork strips look wider is to sew thin cloth strips to each side of the patchwork strip before sewing on the background color strips.*

4-21. *This short Seminole-inspired skirt is a modern version of the gathered, ground-sweeping Seminole patchwork skirts. The single strand of beads is a scant reminder of the pounds of beads that concealed the necks of Seminole women.*

Seminole Patchwork Skirt

The idea for this skirt came from the gathered, floor-length skirts illustrated in Figure 4-2. The skirt is made up of patchwork bands sewn between strips of white cloth.

PATTERN

Use a commercial pattern for a street-length, A-line skirt. Other pattern features include a waistband and side zipper. Or, for a more authentic look, use a pattern for a slightly gathered skirt with a waistband. Length is optional. For either type of skirt, try to find patterns with only two main pattern pieces; that is, one pattern piece for the skirt front and one for the skirt back.

FABRIC

Since producing patchwork is a time-consuming task, you will want results that will last a long time. Buy good-quality fabric to work with. Most Seminole women use cotton or cotton blends, but any smooth good-quality fabric that does not stretch is suitable.

In general, choose light- to meduim-weight fabrics. Heavyweight and stiff fabrics become even stiffer when made into patchwork. Fabric for the patchwork and for the background color strips should be the same or of very similar fabric.

Usually, the solid color bands, or background color strips, sewn between the patchwork bands dictate the overall color scheme of the skirt. Select colors for the patchwork, narrow applique, and rickrack, etc. that coordinate with the background color; or, you may prefer to use a contrasting or even random color arrangement. Common background colors used by Seminole women are blue, red, white, yellow, and black.

I used about 1¼ yards (1.2 m) of white 44/45-inch-wide (115-cm) fabric for background color strips and waistband for this Seminole skirt adaptation.

I have never figured out an absolutely accurate way to predetermine how much fabric is needed to create patchwork bands. For this project, if you are using only three colors, buy at least 1 yard (.9 m) of each. If you are using many colors, ½ yard (.45 m) of each is sufficient.

I used blue, yellow, lime green, and white in the patchwork. The background color strips were white. No narrow applique or rickrack was added.

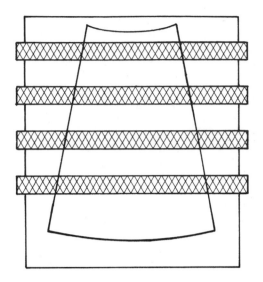

4-22. *Sew patchwork strips (represented by diagonal crosshatch) between background color strips to create enough yardage to cover the skirt pattern pieces.*

SPECIAL INSTRUCTIONS

For this or a floor-length skirt, you will need to complete eight to twelve bands of patchwork. If you are making the A-line, street-length skirt, you will need eight bands—four for the skirt front and four for the skirt back. Make two bands of four different designs. Use your skirt pattern piece as a guide to calculate how long each band should be. The bands in my skirt varied in width from 3 to 5 inches (7.6 to 12.7 cm).

If you are making a floor-length, gathered skirt (as shown in Figure 4-2), you will need twelve bands—six for the front and six for the back. Make two bands of six different designs.

Once you have completed the required number of patchwork bands, lay one of each design below another to check how the bands will look in the skirt. Rearrange them as desired. Cut the background color strips 4½ inches (11.2 cm) wide if you are average height. This measurement includes seam allowances, but if you are exceptionally tall or short, you may want to add to or subtract from this measurement. The bottom band should be 6½ inches (16.2 cm) wide to allow for the hem. Use the skirt pattern piece to determine how long the background color strips need to be.

Using ⅝-inch (1.5-cm) seams, sew the background strips to the patchwork bands. (See Figure 4-22.) You should have two banded pieces—one for the skirt front and one for the skirt back. Make sure that you sew the bands to the background strips in the same order in both front and back pieces. Care must be taken so that the patchwork band seams match when the pieces are cut and sewn together. If you are making the floor-length skirt, the banded pieces will look similar, but will have six bands each. Press all seams toward the bottom of the skirt. Cut the skirt front and skirt back from the banded pieces. Cut the waistband from the background color fabric.

Attach a 7-inch (17.5-cm) zipper in the left seam, ⅝ inch (1.5 cm) below the top. Make sure the patchwork bands line up at the side seam. Hand-baste the remaining left side seam and the right side seam, aligning the patchwork bands. Machine-stitch the side seams and press the seam allowances open. Whether you are making the gathered or the A-line skirt, follow the printed pattern instructions and then attach the waistband and finish the garment.

Seminole One-Band Patchwork Skirt

When the Seminole women began sewing patchwork garments for tourists in the 1940's and 50's, their personal wardrobes suffered. Instead of taking the time to sew fully patchworked skirts, they began making skirts with a single band of patchwork near the bottom. In order to enhance the trim, they added numerous rows of thin, multicolored applique bands and rickrack above and below the patchwork band. This is an excellent time-saving alternative to the multi-banded skirt. Yet it is still authentic and it gives you a chance to attractively display your handiwork.

PATTERN

Select a commercial pattern for a gathered skirt with two main pattern pieces in street or floor length. It should have a side closure and a waistband.

FABRIC

Cotton and cotton blends are the best fabrics, though any smooth, medium-weight fabric will do.

A size 12 street-length, gathered skirt will require about 1½ yards (1.4 m) of 44/45-inch-wide (115-cm) fabric. For the patchwork strip, ⅛- to ¼-yard (11.4- to 22.8-cm) pieces of colored fabric are sufficient, depending upon how many colors you will be using in the design.

SPECIAL INSTRUCTIONS

First make two wide bands of patchwork. Measure horizontally across the lower part of the skirt pattern pieces to determine how long the bands need to be. Cut two 6½-inch-wide (16.2-cm) strips of the background color for the skirt bottom. Sew the bottom strip to the lower edge of one patchwork band. Lay the skirt pattern piece over the two connected bands to determine how large a piece of background color fabric is needed for the top part of the skirt. (See Figure 4-24.) Cut the required length and sew it to the top edge of the patchwork band. You will need two of these banded pieces. Cut out the skirt front from one and the skirt back from the other.

Follow the printed pattern instructions to complete the garment. You should hand-baste the side seams, making sure the patchwork bands match, before stitching with the sewing machine.

4-23. *As Seminole women began sewing more for tourists, in order to save time, they began making one-band Seminole skirts for themselves. The one band is made to look wider by adding many rows of rickrack and thin cloth applique.*

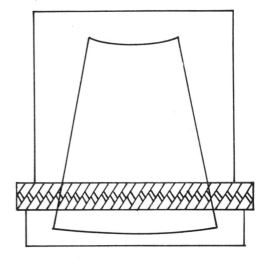

4-24. *Start at the bottom and work up when building yardage for a one-band Seminole patchwork skirt.*

61

4-25. *Seminole patchwork bands can be sewn parallel to the front band of a man's shirt.*

4-26. *Seminole women prefer to sew patchwork bands horizontally across the chest on the men's shirts.*

Seminole Patchwork-Trimmed Shirts

Many of the shirts worn by Seminole men today are trimmed with single patchwork bands, as opposed to being constructed entirely of patchwork. (See Figures 4-25 and 4-26.)

PATTERN

Apply the decorative panels to any ready-made shirt or to any made from a commercial pattern. A basic, button-front shirt with long, cuffed sleeves is commonly used by Seminole women.

FABRIC

Cotton and cotton blends are the best fabrics for this project. Seminole women usually make their men's shirts in light-colored fabric and use darker shades of the same color in the patchwork. Favorite shirt colors are yellow, light blue, and white.

A man's shirt, medium size, will require about 2¼ yards (2.1 m) of 44/45-inch-wide (115-cm) fabric. For the patchwork strips, ⅛- to ¼-yard (11.4- to 22.8-cm) pieces of fabric are sufficient, depending on how many colors you will be using in the patchwork design.

SPECIAL INSTRUCTIONS

First you will need to sew your patchwork bands. Use your printed pattern pieces as a guide to compute how long to make the patchwork bands. (The shirt shown in Figure 4-25 requires longer bands than does the shirt shown in Figure 4-26.)

Lay out and cut all the pattern pieces according to the printed pattern instructions. Position the patchwork bands where desired and use the bias tape method (illustrated in Figure 4-7) to attach the bands to the shirt front pieces. With this method, you lay bias tape over the edges of the positioned patchwork and sew through the tape, the patchwork, and the shirt fronts.

You may also want to add thin patchwork bands, rickrack or thin cloth applique trim to the collar and cuffs. Do so while they are unassembled. When you are satisfied with the trimming you've done follow the printed pattern instructions to complete the shirt.

Seminole Military Coat Adaptation

This military coat adaptation is easy to make and can be a stunning outfit when worn with the appropriate accessories.

PATTERN

There are many commercial patterns for wraparound dresses that would be suitable. To achieve the features you desire, you may have to alter the pattern slightly. Shown

4-27. *This modern adaptation of the military coat in brightly striped Swiss cotton, worn with triple gorgets, is very eye-catching.*

are three coats, each with different, but authentic, design features. Use the drawings to help you select a pattern with the style features you desire. (See Figure 4-28.)

Commercial printed patterns are also available for turbans, or you may want to purchase one ready-made, in a color that complements the coat fabric.

FABRIC

For authenticity, use cotton, but any smooth fabric is suitable. Choose a medium-weight fabric, such as the Swiss cotton I used. The Southeastern tribes used cotton, because it was one of the few fabrics available to them and it was probably the coolest to wear. For the turban, stretch knits work well.

Dark blue and maroon are good authentic colors; fabric striped with these two colors is particularly authentic. Blue with white stripes or pale yellow with tan stripes were popular fabrics too. Prints were often softly colored; some were even of pastel shades. Green and light blue were popular colors in floral-type prints.

My wrap-dress pattern in size 12 required 3⅝ yards (3.3 m) of 44/45-inch-wide (115-cm) fabric. The turban required about 2 yards (1.85 m) of 44/45-inch-wide (115-cm) fabric.

SPECIAL INSTRUCTIONS

Lay out, cut, and assemble the coat pieces according to the printed pattern instructions. Do the same for the turban.

For the wide sash belt, use the same fabric as the coat and cut a piece 76 by 8 inches (190 by 20 cm). Fold the piece in half, right sides of fabric together. Using a ½-inch (1.2-cm) seam, sew one end closed, and sew along the long side toward the center. Break the stitching. Repeat, starting at the other end and leaving a 4-inch (10-cm) opening. Turn the belt right side out, press, and slipstitch the open section closed.

The coat and accessories can be worn with slacks or alone.

4-28. *Collar and sleeve variations for the Seminole military coat. The ruffles can be of the same fabric as the coat or of a different color. Some older garments show white or red ruffles on a blue garment and red ruffles on a green or yellow garment.*

65

5-1. *This photograph shows an Iroquois navy blue wool skirt decorated with tiny white beads sewn into intricate designs. The earlier version of this garment was a brown dyed wraparound leather skirt embroidered with white porcupine quills or moose hair.* Courtesy Denver Art Museum, Denver, Colorado.

5 Iroquois Clothing Styles

THE FIVE NATIONS Iroquoian Confederacy, or the Iroquois people, inhabited a large area stretching from Northern Pennsylvania to the Great Lakes and from Ohio to Vermont. (See the map on page 7.) The five nations were the Mohawk, Oneida, Onondaga, Cayuga, and Seneca. Later, a sixth group, the Tuscarora, joined the Confederacy. These groups were and are culturally similar in many respects. During the Revolutionary War, they sided with the British and, as a result, were later exiled to Canada. Most Iroquoian people still reside in Canada, though remnants of each nation (except the Onondaga) live in New York State.

Onc of thc first clothing styles developed by the Iroquois women was the long wraparound deerskin skirt. Sometimes these were dyed dark brown and decorated with porcupine quill or moose hair embroidery. Contact with Europeans came as early as the 1530's, and trade soon developed, bringing wool and cotton cloth, glass beads, and ribbon to the Iroquois. The women began to use the new materials to make their long wraparound skirts and other clothing styles. (See Figure 5-1.) Also, the decorations that had previously been made with natural products could now be made with beads and accented with ribbons.

5-2. *The Iroquois skirt adapted for contemporary wear. The navy wool skirt is decorated with Iroquois designs executed in white crewel wool with embroidery stitching. The model is wearing an elaborately perforated Iroquois silver brooch.*

The beadwork designs added to garments varied widely. Geometric as well as floral and scroll-type designs were often intermixed in Iroquoian beadwork. The floral designs look very European and were possibly adopted from French missionaries who worked with the Iroquois people from the 1600's on.

Whereas there had been no upper garment in the Iroquois woman's wardrobes up till then, one evolved in the mid-nineteenth century in the form of a long cotton tunic. The front of the costume was taken from the dresses of Anglo women, while the back was adopted from the court coats of Anglo male officials. By combining these different elements, the Iroquois woman created a new garment for herself. The tunics were decorated with ribbons, beadwork, and silver brooches.

By the 1860's, because the majority of the people had accepted Anglo clothing styles, the Iroquois costume was seldom seen, except at festivals. By the 1900's, the prevailing costume worn by Iroquois at festivals and large gatherings was of the Plains Indian style. With the increase in Native American awareness in the past two decades, however, the Iroquois have been trying to recreate their traditional styles. Today, the costumes worn by the Iroquois at special occasions reflect the old, distinctive style and decoration.

Iroquois-Style Skirt

This Iroquois-style skirt, if worn with a plain top, can be an excellent backdrop for silver, especially Iroquois-made silver pieces. The designs decorating the skirt are executed in crewel wool with embroidery stitching.

PATTERN

Use a commercial pattern for a wraparound skirt, street- or floor-length. The overlapping of the front pieces should follow conventional wraparound skirts. A waistband is optional.

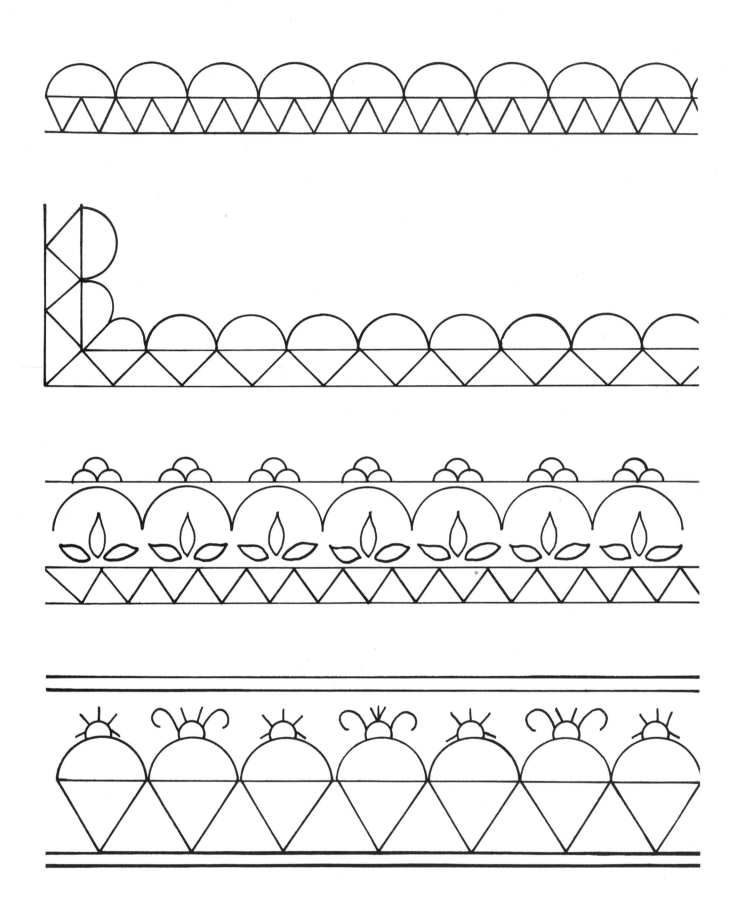

5-3. *Typical Iroquois border decorations.*

FABRIC

Light- to medium-weight wool is what most Iroquois women use. Although knits can be used, you must be careful during the embroidering not to pull too tightly or you will cause ripples and puckers around the design. For my skirt, I used wool fabric and wool crewel embroidery thread.

Recommended skirt colors are black, dark blue, and red. These are colors used by Iroquois women, and, against these dark colors, the white beadwork or embroidery show up clearly.

A street-length wraparound skirt in size 12 will require 1⅝ yards (1.5 m) of 60-inch-wide (150-cm) fabric.

SPECIAL INSTRUCTIONS

You can create the designs for the hem and overflap of the wraparound skirt either by beadwork or embroidery. I recommend the embroidery method because it is easier and much faster. If you are more ambitious and decide to execute the design with beads, look at books on Indian beadwork and check hobby and craft stores for supplies.

To begin this project, first lay out and cut the pattern pieces according to the printed instructions. Sew the skirt front pieces to the back piece(s) at the side seams. Mark the seam line of the edge of the right overlapping skirt front and press and baste the hem in place.

The drawings here are just some of the border and corner designs you might use. (See Figures 5-3 and 5-4.) The corner designs are different representations of the celestial tree which symbolizes the Tree of Life, which, according to Iroquois legend, is said to stand in the center of the world bearing the sun and moon in its branches. For additional Iroquois designs, examine *Iroquois Crafts* by Carrie Lyford.

Once you have selected a border design, enlarge it and transfer a small section of it onto paper. Three of the sample border designs given here (see Figure 5-3) require only one triangle and one dome pattern piece of posterboard or heavy paper. The fourth design requires a leaf pattern also. Use your drawing as a guide to making the pattern pieces you will need. Any embellishments (see the bottommost design) can be done freehand. In the design for my skirt the triangles are 1 inch (2.54 cm) high and the domes are 1¾ inches (4.4 cm) tall, creating a design 2¾ inches (6.94 cm) wide.

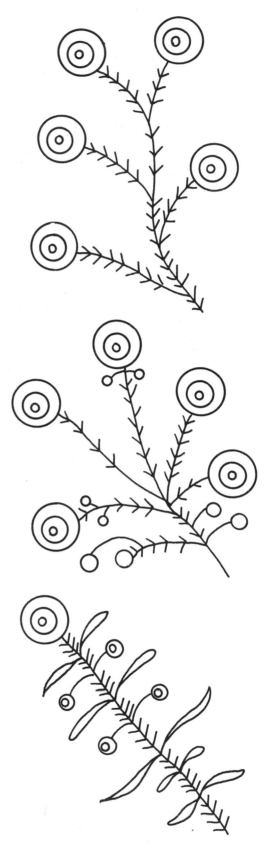

5-4. *Iroquois "Tree of Life" designs.*   71

5-5. *The stem stitch (also called the outline stitch) is recommended for creating Iroquois designs.*

Start marking your design at the corner of the skirt overflap. Using tailor's chalk pencil and a ruler, mark a straight line up the front of the fabric, 1 inch (2.54 cm) inside the seam line. Starting again at the corner point, draw a line around the hem of the skirt about 2½ inches (6.3 cm) above the finished bottom of the skirt. Using this line as a base, use your triangle, dome, and leaf (if appropriate) paper patterns and your ruler to mark the design along the front and bottom edges of the skirt.

Embroider the design using a stem stitch. (See Figure 5-5.) Add the corner design after the borders are finished. Mark the fabric freehand with tailor's chalk pencil and embroider, again using the stem stitch.

Follow the printed pattern instructions to attach the waistband and finish the garment.

Iroquois-Style Blouse

This blouse is one of the more modern Iroquois-style garments. The designs that embellish it are authentic Iroquois shirt decorations. I recommend using embroidery to adorn the garment in place of the beadwork the Iroquois do.

PATTERN

You will need a commercial pattern with the following features: slit-front opening and fairly wide elbow-length, three-quarter-length, or long sleeves. The garment can be a blouse or street- to floor-length dress.

FABRIC

I recommend white or natural color cotton, light- to medium-weight wool or medium- to heavyweight silk for the garment. If you prefer, you can use solid colors or even black fabric. Use brightly colored embroidery floss for the decorations. On wool fabric, you may want to use crewel embroidery wool.

A size 12, hip-length tunic top will require 2 yards (1.85 m) of 44/45-inch-wide (115-cm) fabric.

5-6. *This Iroquois shirt can also be made into a dress. The intricate winding designs originally created with colored beads are just as attractive in colorful embroidery thread.*

SPECIAL INSTRUCTIONS

Lay out and cut the blouse or dress according to the printed pattern instructions. It will be easier to do the embroidery work on the unassembled front piece.

Select a design for the embellishment by using one of those given here or creating your own. (See Figure 5-7.)

Enlarge and transfer your design onto tracing paper. Use an iron-on transfer pencil (available at craft and fabric stores) or your favorite method to transfer the design from paper onto the cloth. Embroider the design in one color, or in many colors, if the design is a floral type. The stem stitch (also called the "outline stitch") (see Figure 5-5) is one you might consider using (see Figure 5-5), or consult any basic craft book or embroidery book for other stitches you might use.

When you have completed the embroidery work, follow the printed pattern instructions to complete the garment. Do not attempt to wear necklaces with this garment. They will compete with the design. However, bracelets will show up nicely.

5-7. *Iroquois-style blouse decoration motifs.*

73

6 Great Lakes Area Clothing Styles

 AS TRADE WITH EUROPEANS became established, almost all tribes had access to ribbons. It was the woodland tribes living in the Great Lakes area and the upper Mississippi Valley, however, that developed a unique and complex method to turn ribbons into colorful decorative panels to add to their clothing. (See the map on page 7.)

The evolution of the Native Americans' use of ribbon as clothing decoration can be traced back centuries. Porcupine quills were the first step in the evolution. The quills were dyed and worked into decorative, usually geometric, symmetrical panels on shirts, skirts, leggings, and shawls.

The white man introduced glass beads to the tribes of the Northeast and Canada in the seventeenth century, and this led to the development of intricate, painstakingly fashioned beadwork. The Native Americans mastered this craft and used it to decorate clothing, moccasins, leather bags, bracelets, necklaces, and hair ornaments. The beads were easier to work with than were the quills, and floral designs in addition to geometric ones began to appear.

When muslin and other light cloths became available, they were used in place of tanned hides to make certain garments. Traded along with the cloth were ribbons, and, by the late eighteenth century, both cloth and ribbon were

6-1. *Native American women of the Great Lakes area originally made their men leather shirts, which were decorated with porcupine quills and moose hair, and later, with glass beads when they became available. When cotton cloth arrived they moved their beaded strips onto shirts made of cloth, shown here.* Courtesy Denver Art Museum, Denver, Colorado.

6-2. *As time passed, the beaded strips, which were often outlined with ribbon, were dropped and simulated by stitched tucks of fabric outlined with ribbon.* Courtesy Denver Art Museum, Denver, Colorado.

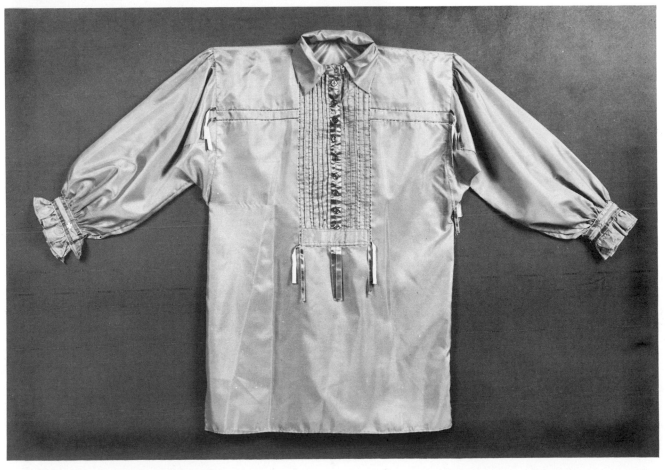

commonly available. Use of ribbon was especially accepted by woodland tribes living from the Great Lakes south to Oklahoma.

Shirts were some of the first garments to be made from cloth. The seamstresses did their beadwork on the cotton shirts and used the colorful ribbon as borders, especially around beaded strips, which were placed along the shoulder seams and down the front of the shirt. (See Figure 6-1.)

In time, many seamstresses began eliminating the beaded strips and applied only the ribbons. The beaded panels were replaced or simulated by pleated and tucked chest panels. (See Figure 6-2.) Modern versions of these shirts often do not even have the pleated sections.

The common name for the resulting garment is the "ribbon shirt," which is also called *bethaquah*. The modern ribbon shirt is widely used among Native Americans throughout the United States as part of the contemporary dance costume, and many of the young have adopted the garment as a symbol of pride in their ancestry.

Old photographs show a distinct type of ribbon shirt worn mostly by older men. It is still worn today. The shirt is of black cloth, trimmed with ribbon pieces in three to five colors. The ribbon pieces are attached in the back yoke. The ribbons in the back yoke can be from 3 to 5 inches (7.5 to 13 cm) long. Two colors of ribbon, side by side or lapped, are attached over the shoulder seams and are long enough to dangle loosely 4 to 6 inches (10 to 15.2 cm) down over the arm. Given here is a sketch of this somber but distinguished and striking garment. (See Figure 6-3, and for a modern adaptation, Figure 6-9.)

Another more complex way of using ribbon to decorate garments is "ribbon applique." This art form also used floral and geometric patterns originally produced with quills and beads. The designs are mostly symmetrical patterns done in at least two colors of ribbon, each side a different color. Some Native American women use as many as a dozen ribbons in as many different colors to create complex and beautiful motifs. Only the simplest designs and methods will be discussed here.

This type of ribbonwork is more common to Great Lakes area tribes, but was practiced to a small extent by some tribes in the Northeast and the Southeast. It is believed to have begun in the mid-eighteenth century. As tribes that developed the craft were forced west by whites, they introduced it to the Middle and Southern Plains people.

6-3. *Older men of Native American descent prefer to wear ribbon shirts made of black fabric decorated with colored ribbon sewn along the shoulders and into the back yoke seam.*

Ribbonwork was originally done with silk ribbons, but these are virtually unobtainable in the United States today. Recently, silk, nylon, satin, and rayon purchased as yard goods and cut as needed, have been used. At first, all ribbonwork was done by hand, often with a contrasting color of thread and a decorative cross or herringbone stitch. Today, most ribbonwork is done by machine, often with a zigzag stitch. Then and now, blindstitching by hand is most often done to attach the ribbonwork panel to the garment.

There are two ways to create ribbon applique. These can be referred to as "cut ribbonwork" and "applique ribbonwork." To illustrate, shown here are three ribbon squares. (See Figure 6-4.) A small circle is cut out of the black square. If the cutout circle were to be sewn on one of the pieces of white ribbon, the result would be applique ribbonwork (center). If the black ribbon minus the cutout circle were to be placed over the other piece of white ribbon, the result would be cut ribbonwork.

6-4. *To illustrate the two types of ribbonwork, we start with one square of black ribbon and two squares of white ribbon. A circle has been cut from the center of the black ribbon square. When the black circle is sewn into one of the white ribbon squares you have created an example of applique ribbonwork. When the black ribbon square with the circle cut out is sewn over the other white ribbon square, an example of cut ribbonwork has been created.*

77

6-5. *Great Lakes women excelled in producing beautiful and intricate ribbonwork. This young girl of the Osage tribe wears a robe decorated with bold, geometric ribbonwork.* Courtesy Smithsonian Institution, National Anthropological Archives, Photo. No. T-13, 409.

There are innumerable patterns, certain types being characteristic of specific tribes. (See Figure 6-5.) Today, these designs are still used on traditional costumes, usually for dance.

Though Native American women usually reserve use of their ribbon applique garments for festivals and pow-wows, certain members of the woodland tribes have begun to produce skirts and other garments for commercial sale, using these attractive and colorful designs.

Great-Lakes-Style Ribbon Shirt

The ribbon shirt is one of the most popular of contemporary Native American garments. It is also one of the easiest to make, and it is suitable for men and women. Figure 6-6 illustrates only two of the myriad ways to decorate shirts with ribbons. The arrangement of the ribbons are copied from Native American seamstresses but your choice of fabric and colors of ribbon makes the garment a personal statement.

6-6. *Only two of the myriad of ways in which ribbons can be used to decorate shirts. The shirt style at the left is the most popular for ribbon shirts. The yoked shirt at the right is less common, but particularly suitable if you want free hanging ribbons attached into the yoke seams.*

6-7. *Patterns for ribbon shirts.*

PATTERN

The original shirts made by Native American women were very simple, and modern ribbon-shirt makers tend to follow the trend. Use a commercial pattern for a very simple, vertical front-slit opening, cuffed sleeve, and collared shirt. A pattern with an underarm gusset would be very authentic. Given here are some sketches of some basic ribbon shirt patterns generally used.

FABRIC

You can use almost any smooth fabric, printed or in solid colors. The prints used by Native Americans vary from stripes, polka dots, and florals, to Mickey and Minnie Mouse designs. Most ribbon shirts are of cotton or cotton blends, but I have seen examples in which satin, in solid colors, small floral prints, or stripes, was used.

The ribbons can be grosgrain or of the shiny synthetic variety. Most Native American women use the shiny type. The color(s) can match or contrast with the color(s) of the fabric and you can apply them in a multitude of ways. The ribbon shirt on the left in Figure 6-6 requires 2 yards (1.85 m) of 44/45-inch-wide (115-cm) fabric for a size 12 garment. The ribbon shirt on the right requires 2¼ yards (2.1 m) of fabric.

I used 2 yards (1.85 m) each of ⅝-inch-wide (1.5 cm) red and black ribbon to decorate the shirt on the left. The shirt on the right, which has long ribbons hanging from the center of the back yoke, as well as the front ones, re-

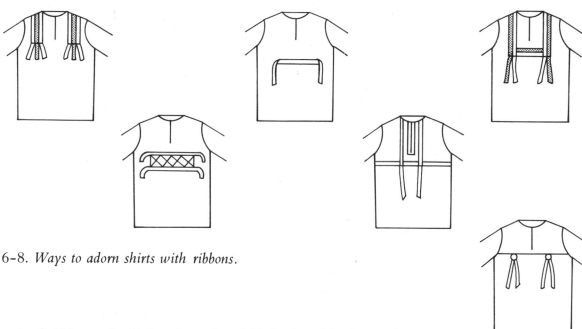

6-8. *Ways to adorn shirts with ribbons.*

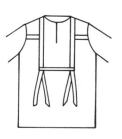

quired 1⅜ yards (1.3 m) each of ⅜-inch-wide (9-mm) green and red ribbon. Each set of dangling ribbons consists of one red and one green ribbon and is 16 inches (40.6 cm) long.

SPECIAL INSTRUCTIONS

Follow the printed pattern instructions to lay out and cut the pattern pieces. The examples given here are exact duplicates of ribbon shirts decorated by Native Americans of different tribes. Select an arrangement of ribbons you like and, using a pencil and ruler, draw the placement of the ribbons on the cut pattern piece. Should you use a pattern with a collar, consider adding one or two ribbons to it. Also, Native American women often decorate cuffs with one or more ribbons. If you are ambitious, you may want to produce thin ribbon applique (see page 77) to attach to your ribbon shirt. Notice that many of the examples leave portions of the ribbons dangling. The ribbons flutter with any movement.

Sew the ribbons to the garment pieces. Stitch both edges of the ribbon and then follow printed pattern instructions to complete the garment.

The slit- or tab-front closings are excellent for wearing with chokers and long necklaces. If made long enough, the shirt could be worn loose, tucked in, or belted. You may want to use silver, abalone, mother-of-pearl, or deer horn buttons for tab and cuff closings. These are available in Native American supply stores.

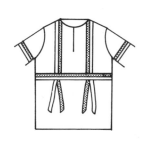

6-9. *This black top has been decorated with purple, lilac, aqua, and turquoise ribbons. The slacks are made of the same fabric as the top and together they create an attractive outfit.*

Great-Lakes-Style Ribbon Shirt Outfit

A variation of the colorful ribbon shirt popular among young Native Americans is the somber black ribbon shirt sometimes worn by older men of Native American descent. To offset the somberness of the black shirt, colorful ribbons are sewn along the shoulder seams and tucked into the back yoke seam. A very attractive outfit is created by making slacks or a long skirt of the same fabric as the shirt.

PATTERN

Choose a commercial pattern for a shirt with a vertical front-slit opening, cuffed sleeve, collar, and a back yoke. If you are making a complete outfit, choose for the bottom half, a slacks or long, slim skirt pattern.

FABRIC

If you are making just the shirt, cotton or any smooth fabric will do. For my outfit I used a heavy polyester satin with a dull sheen. This is an excellent choice because it is attractive, washable, and it is heavy enough for the slacks and skirt.

Use the shiny-type ribbons. Any colors are suitable, although red and yellow are usually among those favored by Native American seamstresses. Use at least three different colors. I used two shades of turquoise in ⅝-inch-wide (1.5-cm) ribbon for the shoulder seams and a combination of the turquoise and two shades of purple ribbon in ⅝-inch- and ¼-inch-widths (1.5-cm and 6-mm) in the back yoke.

A size 12 black ribbon shirt requires 2 yards (1.85 m) of 44/45-inch-wide (115-cm) fabric. Slacks will require 2½ yards (2.3 m) of fabric. To decorate the shirt, I used 1 yard (.9 m) each of ⅝-inch-wide (1.5-cm) purple and aqua ribbon, 1¾ yards (1.6 m) of ⅝-inch-wide (1.5-cm) turquoise ribbon and 1 yard (.9 m) each of ¼-inch-wide (6-mm) lilac and aqua ribbon.

SPECIAL INSTRUCTIONS

Lay out and cut pattern pieces from the black fabric, according to printed pattern instructions. Cut pieces of ribbon for the back yoke in 3- to 5-inch (7.5- to 13-cm) lengths. Baste the ribbon pieces to the shirt back where the back yoke will be sewn. (See Figure 6–3.) The ribbons should be basted vertically. They look angled in the drawing to show that they are free hanging. Place the ribbons no less than ¾ inch (1.8 cm) apart. You can use several colors of single ribbon pieces in ⅝-inch (1.5-cm) widths, or do as I did and center a ¼-inch (6-mm) ribbon piece in a light shade over a ⅝-inch (1.5-cm) piece of darker colored ribbon. I alternated the shades of purple with the shades of turquoise. Once your yoke ribbons are basted in place, sew the back yoke to the shirt back.

Sew the shirt back to the shirt front at the shoulder seams. Measure the length of the shoulder seam and add 4 to 6 inches (10 to 15.2 cm). Cut two colors of ribbon for each shoulder seam. Lay the ribbons side by side, one over the other, or one lapped half over the other. Starting at the neck edge, sew the ribbons over the shoulder seams to within 1 inch (2.5 cm) of the edge where the sleeve will be attached. It is a good idea to fold back and baste the free-hanging part of the ribbon so that it will not be accidently sewn into the sleeve or collar seams. Follow the printed pattern instructions to complete the garment. Follow the printed pattern instructions to construct the slacks or long skirt.

Cut all free-hanging ribbon ends at a 45-degree angle to help retard unraveling.

Great-Lakes-Style Ribbonwork Caftan

Ribbonwork decorations were originally used on shirts, skirts, leggings, shawls, and moccasins. A beautifully decorated shawl, dating back to approximately 1904, is pictured earlier. (See Figure 6–5.) In this project I have decorated a caftan with ribbonwork. (See Figure 6–10.)

6-10. *Ribbonwork panels have been attached to a caftan in this contemporary use of an old decorative art.*

PATTERN

Since the main feature of this Native-American-influenced fashion idea is in the form of a decorative panel or strip, you can use any pattern that can accommodate these decorative features. You may want to purchase a ready-made garment and add the ribbonwork to it.

The ribbonwork decorated skirts made by Great Lakes Indian women are particularly lovely. On a gathered skirt, a strip made of four widths of ribbon forms a wide panel down the front, while just above the hem, a strip of two widths of ribbon decorates the skirt all the way around.

FABRIC

You can attach the ribbonwork panels to garments of any smooth medium- to heavyweight fabric.

Most Native American women use the shiny type of ribbon in 2-¼-inch (5.7-cm) width. For very wide panels, buy satin, silk, or taffeta by the yard. Most Native American women clip and then tear the fabric into appropriate widths to ensure straight pieces. Alternatively, you can use a yardstick taped to a cardboard grid-marked cutting board. Line up the fabric to a grid line and use the yardstick to guide the scissors as you cut.

Predominant ribbon colors seen in Native American creations are blue, purple, orange, and green. For this caftan I chose lilac and purple. Native American women often use two shades of one color, although almost any two colors can be mixed and will still create pleasing results.

You will need ribbon in two colors, each 2¼ inches (5.7 cm) wide (or, whatever you choose, but this is a good width with which to work), a third color of narrower ribbon (usually black) to be used for bordering the ribbonwork, thread to match each ribbon color, and posterboard for the design pattern.

This caftan in size 12 required 4⅝ yards (4.2 m) of 44/45-inch-wide (115-cm) fabric. For the ribbon work panels I used 2½ yards (2.3 m) each of 2¼-inch-wide (5.7-cm) lilac and purple ribbon. To outline the panels I needed 2½ yards (2.3 m) of ⅝-inch-wide (1.5-cm) black ribbon.

SPECIAL INSTRUCTIONS

Lay out and cut the pattern pieces of the garment according to the printed pattern instructions. It will be easier to attach the ribbonwork panels to the unassembled cloth pattern pieces.

Select a design pattern from those given here. (See Figure 6-11.) Enlarge and transfer to a piece of posterboard. A 3- by 11-inch (7.5-by 28-cm) of posterboard is a good general size, but, of course, the design can be enlarged or reduced as desired. Use the topmost pattern given here to help visualize how the rest of the designs will look when completed. If you choose to use the topmost design, you will need to cut two pattern pieces—the black portion of the double-headed arrow and the black portions of the hearts. If you choose to use the bottommost design, you will also need two pattern pieces—the black sawtooth piece and the small wedgelike piece. The two center designs require only one pattern piece each.

To make the panels, cut two pieces of the 2¼-inch-wide (5.7-cm) ribbon in each color (for purposes of visualization, Color A and Color B) to the length needed. If you are using cut yard goods in place of ribbons, you will need to calculate an additional ½ inch (1.2 cm) into the desired width. Turn and press ¼-inch (6-mm) hems along both sides of your "ribbon" before you begin to sew. Place one Color A ribbon over the entire length of a Color B ribbon and baste them together along the edges. Repeat this procedure with the second ribbon lengths, reversing, and place Color B over Color A. Loosely catch-stitch the two ribbon lengths together, edges touching, but not overlapping. (See Figure 6-12.)

6-11. *Ribbonwork designs suitable for enlarging. Make a pattern of heavy paper. On any ribbonwork design, your paper pattern is actually only half of the complete design. The top, left sample illustrates how the complete design will look.*

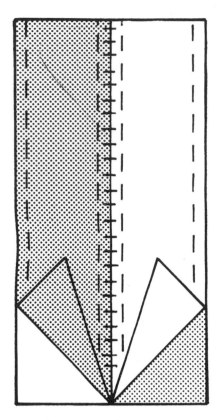 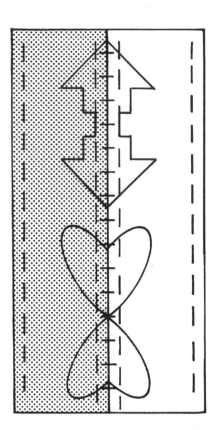 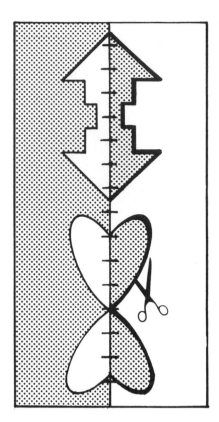

6-12. *To create ribbonwork panels, first baste two sets of ribbons, one on top of the other. Catch-stitch the two-layered ribbon pieces together, colors alternating as shown.*

6-13. *Use your paper pattern to trace the design on both colors of ribbon.*

6-14. *Stitch along the traced design line and cut away the top ribbon only.*

Determine how many complete pattern motifs can be traced along the ribbon length, so that each motif is touching or equally spaced and the space left over at each end is equal. Mark one end where the last motif ends as a starting point for tracing. Place the paper pattern on one ribbon at the marked end and trace with a pencil. Flop the paper pattern over onto the adjoining ribbon and trace the motif again. Repeat, tracing both sides of the motif along the entire length of each ribbon, each tracing equally spaced from the next. (See Figure 6-13.)

Using thread that matches the top ribbon, zigzag-stitch or satin-stitch along the inside of each traced line. With small, sharp scissors, cut away the top ribbon only along the outside of the stitching. (See Figure 6-14.)

When finished, a positive-negative design is created. Slipstitch the two strips together in place of the loose catch stitches and remove the catch stitches. You may find it

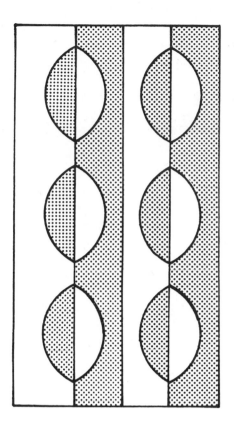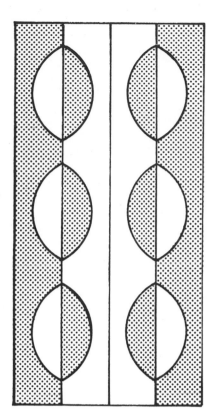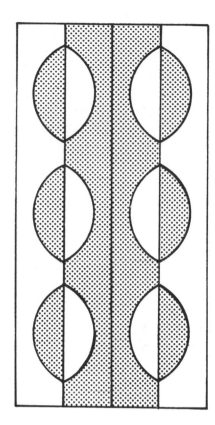

6–15. *For very wide ribbonwork panels, there are many ways to vary the look by changing the order of the ribbon colors. Shown are some of the ways you can position the different colors of ribbons.*

easier to place the two strips together in position on the garment piece and then slipstitch them together, catching in the fabric of the garment piece.

For wider panels, cut four pieces each of both colors of ribbons. (See Figure 6–15 for different ways to arrange the various colors of ribbon.)

Baste the ribbon panel edges to the garment piece. Using the third color of ribbon and slightly overlapping the ribbonwork, sew the border around the edges.

For my caftan I made three 14-inch-long (35.5-cm) ribbonwork panels. I positioned two panels parallel to the front slit and the third one across their bottoms. I then covered all edges with ⅝-inch (1.5-cm) black ribbon.

On your project, you will then need to trim any excess ribbonwork panel to conform to the edges of the cloth pattern pieces. Finally, complete the garment following the printed pattern instructions.

7 Plains Tribes Clothing Styles

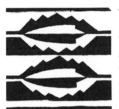 THE TERM PLAINS TRIBESPEOPLE, as used in this book, refers to Native Americans living in the Great Plains area, which reaches from the Mississippi to the Rockies between Texas and the southern parts of Alberta and Saskatchewan, Canada. (See the map on page 7.) Tribes in this area have many clothing styles in common.

At the mention of American Indian, or Native American, the heavily beaded and fringed leather garments of the Plains tribes immediately spring to mind. Plains tribal clothing styles have become the dominant image of "Indianness." This popularity is due partly to the traveling Medicine Shows of the 1800's, which took place throughout the United States and Europe. The image is strengthened by movies and television and the current Pan Indian movement.

The beautiful and colorful Plains-style clothes have been highly publicized and are popular favorites among whites and Native Americans.

Fringes are graceful, eye-catching, and lively additions to the Plains-style costume, but for various reasons have not been widely used in American fashion. One problem has to do with fabric. While leather, traditionally used, fringes beautifully, woven materials merely unravel.

7-1. *One type of skin dress worn by the women of some Plains tribes.* Courtesy Denver Art Museum, Denver, Colorado.

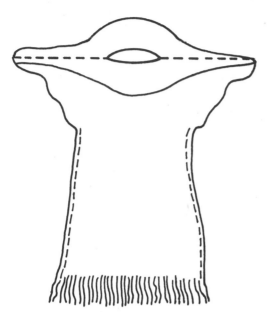

7-2. One common Plains skin dress style had no true sleeve, but merely the appearance of sleeves. The dotted line represents the shoulder seam. The wide "seam allowances" fell forward and back and were often fringed and beaded.

7-3. This elegantly simple wool dress decorated with cowry shells was made in the 1870's by a Sioux woman. There are tie-dye-effect selvages on sleeve ends. Courtesy Denver Art Museum, Denver, Colorado.

A basic garment among the Plains tribes was the "skin dress." (See Figure 7-1.) The pattern was largely dictated by the size and shape of the animal skins from which they were made, but it was usually an A-line dress with full, wide "sleeves." The sleeves were not true sleeves, but loose flaps that looked like sleeves when worn. Given here is an illustration of how front and back skins of a commonly used style has a shoulder seam. (See Figure 7-2.) The extra skin or seam allowance was allowed to fall forward and back. Parts of the extra skin would be fringed, or fringes were added where wanted. Often these "sleeves" were called "butterfly sleeves."

Contrary to popular belief, these dresses were not made from buffalo hide. It would have been too thick and stiff for wear, even when tanned. On the contrary, skin dresses were made from deer, elk, and antelope hides. Different tribes or different factions of one tribe varied the shape of the sleeves and the cut of the dress bottom and would decorate the dress in various ways. Fringes, elk teeth, cowry and dentalium shells, and beadwork were common decorative attachments. (Even before the coming of the Europeans, there was well-established trading with coastal tribes for shells.)

As manufactured cloth was introduced, it was eagerly substituted for hide, but the basic cut of garments remained the same. One of the first imported fabrics was Stroud cloth (from Stroud, England). Often called "strouding," the wool, available in blue, black, red, yellow, and green, was heavy with a harsh texture. It was so thick and tightly woven that it looked like it could easily carry water. The selvages were white and often some dye crept into them, giving the edges a tie-dye-like effect. Stroud cloth can be identified by these unique selvages, and most Native American women used the selvages as sleeve and hem edges. Examples of Stroud cloth dresses exist in many museums.

Before the practice of lining wool had been conceived, some Plains tribal women wore underdresses, usually of calico-type cotton, similar to the practice and style of the Pueblo women, as a soft shield against the harsh wool. In winter the underdress probably added extra protection against the cold, which was especially needed because of the wide butterfly sleeves.

As more trade items were introduced by the Europeans, the women began to use beads and ribbons to decorate their garments.

(A word of caution about using these dresses to show off jewelry is needed. The three-quarter- or elbow-length sleeves make the garment suitable for wearing with bracelets, but, since the dresses themselves are trimmed so heavily, the amount and type of jewelry that can be worn with them is limited.)

At one time, elk's teeth attached to a dress were an indication of the wearer's social status. Only two of the teeth of the elk were considered appropriate for personal adornment, so a woman's provider had to be a skilled hunter to provide her with enough of these particular teeth to decorate an entire dress. Real elk's teeth are virtually unobtainable today, but, even in olden days, some Native American men carved replicas of the teeth from bone for their women's use. Today, replicas of carved bone or molded plastic are available from Native American supply stores.

Since cowry shells are similar to elk's teeth in color and size, some Native American women used them as a substitute. Predrilled cowry shells can be purchased from Native American supply stores and shell stores for pennies apiece. They are usually attached in a circular or straight-across pattern. They can be attached to the bodice only or can cover the entire dress, sleeves included.

Another garment very popular among Plains Indian women was the wool dress decorated with white dentalium shells. Rows and rows of dentalium shells were sewn onto the dress starting at the neck edge and sometimes extending to the elbows. (See Figures 7-3 and 7-4.)

Dentalium shells are also available from Native American supply and shell stores. More expensive than cowry shells, dentalia are slightly curved, thin, long cone-shaped shells. There are two types of dentalia commonly available for purchase. The smooth, thick ones are the type used by Native Americans. In recent times, thin-shelled and slightly ridged dentalia have been imported from Japan. Either type is suitable, and the Japanese ones are less expensive.

7-4. *Two Dakota Indians are wearing dentalium-shell-decorated wool dresses in this photograph taken in 1904. Most Native American children wore clothes that were miniature versions of what the adults wore.* Courtesy Smithsonian Institution National Anthropological Archives. Photo. No. T-25, 904.

Plains-Style Fringe-Decorated Skirt

This modification is made of wool and leather fringes with large beads as the decorations. The fringes can be arranged in many different patterns. Since these are attached with thread loops, they can easily be rearranged or removed for cleaning the skirt.

PATTERN

Select a commercial pattern for a street- or floor-length, flaired skirt or dress. The pattern I used for the skirt has four gores and measures 95 inches (240 cm) around the bottom width. A good bottom width measurement for a street-length skirt is 71 inches (180 cm).

FABRIC

I recommend middle- to heavyweight fabrics because of the weight of the decorations. You may prefer to use a synthetic suede cloth. Keep in mind, however, that any holes made in synthetic suede cloth are permanent, so there will be no allowance for rearrangement. The garment could be made from leather, but special techniques are needed to work with leather, and leather is very expensive. Also keep in mind that caring for leather can be bothersome and expensive. For those interested in using leather, patterns, special instructions, tools, and leather are available at leather and craft stores.

Wool is the fabric I used and it is the best fabric for this project. A size 12 knee-length skirt will require approximately 1⅜ yards (1.3 m) of 60-inch-wide (150-cm) fabric. A size 12 floor-length skirt will require approximately 2⅛ yards (2 m) of 60-inch-wide (150-cm) fabric.

For the fringes, I used suede laces, which are ⅜ inch (9 mm) wide and about 45 inches (114 cm) long. When knotted over the thread loops, the double fringes hang slightly less than half the original measurement. The suede is very supple, as opposed to other types of leather thongs or strips, which are stiff and tend to curl. Suede laces are available in a wide variety of colors and are sold in precut lengths or by the yard. The beads to string on the fringes are available in various colors and sizes. Suede laces and beads are available in craft, hobby, and Native American supply stores. Some fabric stores also sell these. The large beads through which the suede lace will pass are called

7-5. *This dark green wool skirt with brown suede fringes and light green crow beads is an easily made, but attractive, adaptation of the fringed garments of the Great Plains Indians.*

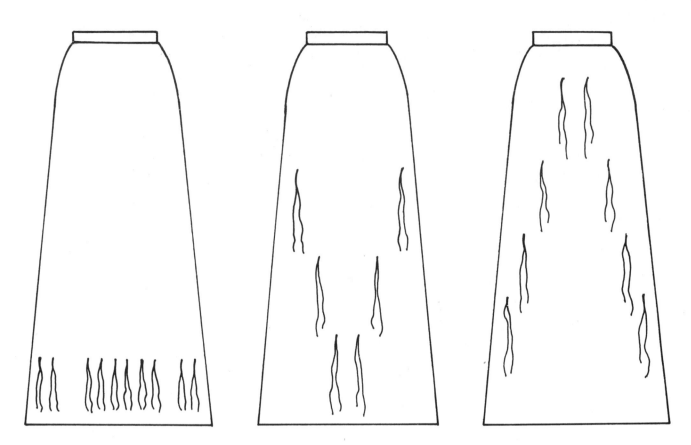

7-6. *Possible arrangements for fringe decoration.*

"crow beads." The beads may stay where placed or, if necessary, knots can be tied below them to hold them in position.

SPECIAL INSTRUCTIONS

Lay out and cut the pattern pieces of the skirt as detailed in the printed pattern instructions. Completely assemble the skirt, including hemming to your desired length.

These fringes are attached through thread loops. This nonpermanent attachment allows for easy removal for cleaning and for rearranging fringes.

Shown here are various patterns into which fringes can be arranged. These arrangements were inspired by actual Native-American-made skin dresses. Choose the pattern of fringe arrangement you prefer. Using a tailor's chalk pencil, lightly mark dots where the thread loops should be made. Measure with a ruler to make sure they are evenly spaced. Use the vertical seams and the skirt bottom as points from which to measure. Once you are satis-

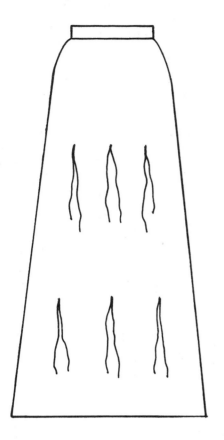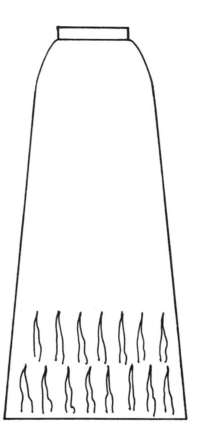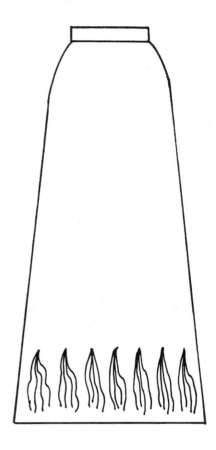

fied with your arrangement, hand-stitch ½-inch-wide (1.2-cm) thread loops. Make them eight threads strong, using thread the same color as your fabric.

On my skirt there are twelve fringes, each 45 inches (114 cm) long. When knotted over the thread loops, they hang 22 inches (56 cm) long. I scwed the thread loops at the two side seams and the center front and center back seams. I placed two loops on each gore, evenly spaced between the seam loops. Note that the fringes hang from almost the middle of the skirt and sweep a few inches above the hem. If you are making a street-length skirt or want to use an arrangement more suitable to shorter fringes, use fringes about 24 inches (60 cm) long, which, when properly attached, will hang about 11 inches (27.5 cm) long. It has been my experience that fringes any shorter do not hang well.

To attach the fringes to the thread loops follow the diagram given here. Decorate the fringes with the desired number and color of crow beads.

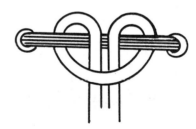

7-7. *Knotting the suede laces over the thread loops in this manner is a secure and neat-looking way to attach decorative fringes.*

Plains-Style Cowry-Shell-Decorated Outfit

This top and the long, slim skirt are adapted from the Plains cowry shell dress pictured in Figure 7-3. The pre-drilled cowry shells are easily attached by hand using a needle and thread. You can determine how many rows of shells to add for yourself. If you make a dress, you may want to scatter shells over the entire garment, as would any proud Native American woman of the Plains.

PATTERN

The commercial pattern used for the top has no separate sleeves. The neckline can be jewel or bateau. This adaptation can be made into a top to be worn with slacks or skirt, or it can be made into a dress of any length.

The basic dress pattern is given here. A pattern with side panel or gusset is very authentic. Many Native American women leave the sleeve seams open and trim them on the three free edges with ribbon. The resulting fluttering attachments deserve the name butterfly sleeves.

FABRIC

I recommend medium- to heavyweight cloth, such as corduroy, velveteen, velvet, or wool. The weight of attachments will pull lightweight fabrics out of shape. "Skin dresses" being made today are usually of wool or corduroy and dark colors, particularly navy blue, red, maroon, or dark green, are preferred by Native American women.

A size 12 top using the pattern given here requires 1¾ yards (1.6 m) of 44/45-inch-wide (115-cm) fabric. A size 12 skirt similar to the one I used requires 2⅜ yards (2.2 m) of 44/45-inch-wide (115-cm) fabric.

SPECIAL INSTRUCTIONS

Lay out and cut the pattern pieces following the printed pattern instructions. Attach the front and back pieces of the top or dress at the shoulders and leave the side seams

7-8. Three rows of cowry shells add interest to the plain lines of this top. The skirt is of the same fabric.

open. If your pattern has separate sleeve pieces, attach them to the armhole edges. Mark shell placement with a chalk fabric-marking pencil. I placed shells approximately 2½ inches (6.2 cm) apart vertically and 2 inches (5 cm) apart horizontally. To get the offset effect, mark one shell place in the first row on the center front, while on the second row, place marks 1 inch (2.54 cm) to either side of center front. On the third row, again place a mark on the center front. Finish marking the front and continue around to the back.

To attach shells, or imitation elk's teeth (if you can find them), use a heavy thread, such as buttonhole twist, and a sharp needle. Choose a thread with a cottonlike finish, as opposed to a satiny synthetic finish, as the former will give better hold when attaching the slippery cowry shells.

Predrilled cowry shells and imitation elk's teeth have only one hole. To attach shells, place one over the chalk mark and bring the needle up through the hole in the shell. Pass it over the shell horizontally and down through the fabric to one side. Repeat four times, if using a single strand of thread; repeat twice, if using double strands of thread. After the fourth stitch, bring the thread up through the shell hole and across horizontally to the other side of the shell and secure with four stitches. (See Figure 7-10.) Because of the somewhat curved shape of the shell, it may slip down somewhat and dangle slightly. This is to be expected.

After all the shells are attached, close the side seams and finish the garment. Cut and construct the slim skirt as detailed in the printed pattern instructions. The pattern I used had a 15-inch (38-cm) slit in the lower left side seam. I sewed five cowry shells 3 inches (7.6 cm) apart along the slit.

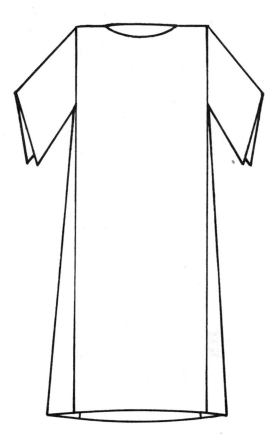

7-9. *Plains cloth dress pattern.*

7-10. *Sew predrilled cowry shells and elk's teeth to garments using a minimum of eight strands of thread.*

7-11. *This adaptation of the trade cloth dentalium-shell-decorated dress is made of velveteen.*

Plains-Style Dentalium-Shell-Decorated Dress

The velveteen dress with dentalium shell-decorated neckline pictured here was inspired by the Plains dress shown in Figure 7-3. Some Native American women attached the shells directly to the garments, while others attached them to a separate piece of fabric and then attached the shell-decorated piece to the basic garment. In either case, many hours are required to sew on the shells. I recommend that you sew your shells onto a separate piece, so, that the basic garment can be cleaned when needed without undue complications.

PATTERN

Choose a commercial pattern for a floor-length, A-line dress with jewel neckline and long, wide uncuffed sleeves. A pattern incorporating the style features illustrated in Figure 7-3 would be suitable also.

FABRIC

I used peacock-colored velveteen for my adaptation. Other suitable fabrics are wool, corduroy, and velvet. The white dentalium shells need a dark background, so I recommend dark colors for the garment. Navy blue was a favorite color among women of the Plains tribes.

A size 12 dress similar to the one I made, will require 4½ years (4.2 m) of velveteen 45 inches (115 cm) wide.

The shells used for my dress were purchased from a Native American supply house in 200-count packages. There are approximately 380 shells on the dress. The shells are natural tubes, but there may be a few in a package that have an extremely small hole in the pointed end. These will need to be clipped so the needle can pass through.

As with the cowries, the number to attach depends on individual taste and may vary from a few to a dozen rows of shells. The shells are arranged in a capelike pattern over the shoulders and can extend partly down the arms as illustrated in Figure 7-3.

SPECIAL INSTRUCTIONS

Lay out and cut the pattern pieces according to the printed pattern instructions. Attach the zipper in the center back seam and sew the front to the backs at the shoulder seams. Finish the neckline by either cutting off the seam allowance and encasing the raw edge with seam binding, or by stay-stitching, then clipping to the stitching and turning the seam allowance to the inside and stitching it down. If you are lining the garment, finish the neck edge by sewing the lining to the garment along the neck seam.

To make a base for the dentalium shell collar, start with the pattern you have chosen for the garment. The width of the collar will vary according to the size of dentalia you have purchased and the number of rows you intend to attach. For purposes of illustration, the procedure for making the garment I made will be explained.

The longest shells were 1⅝ inches (4.2 cm) long, so, for two rows of shells, the collar had to be 3¼ inches (8.2 cm) wide. Add to this the ½ inch (1.2 cm) to be turned under when blindstitching. Then measure 3¾ inches (9.4 cm) from the neck seam at several points and mark the pattern pieces for garment front and garment back. (See Figure 7-12.) Connect the marks. In order to avoid destroying the dress pattern piece, trace the newly marked out pattern piece on tissue paper before cutting. (See Figure 7-13.)

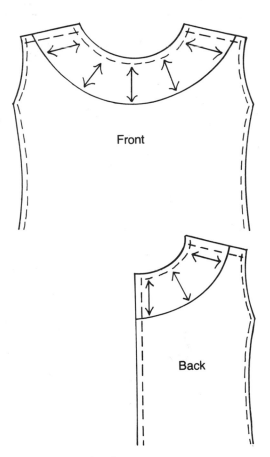

7-12. *Use the dress pattern pieces to make a pattern for the dentalium shell base. Measure out from the neck seam at several points and mark with dots. Then connect the dots.*

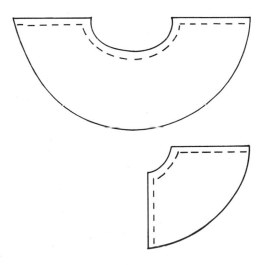

7-13. *Trace the newly marked pattern piece onto tissue paper.*

Cut out the collar base using the same fabric as that of the garment. Also cut interfacing (not fusible type), which will help support the weight of the shells. Cut out the neck facings, which should be among the purchased pattern pieces. Baste the interfacing to the back of the collar pieces. Sew the shoulder seams of the collar and the neck facings. (See Figure 7-14.) Next, sew the collar to the facings, right sides together, around the neck opening. Trim seam allowances and clip curves. Understitch the facing, near the neck seam line, catching in seam allowances. (See Figure 7-15.) Leaving the interfacing free, finish the edges of the collar with overstitching, zigzag-stitching, or pinking shears to prevent unraveling while the shells are being attached.

The shells in a package will vary somewhat in length and it is a good idea to lay them all out in order of length before starting to attach them. Place the largest shells in the center front and the gradually smaller ones over the shoulders and at the back. Attach the shells using a number 16 beading needle. The thread color can either be white or the color of the fabric. Start at one of the back edges of the collar, beginning ⅝ inch (1.5 cm) from the edge, and place the small end of the shell near the neck

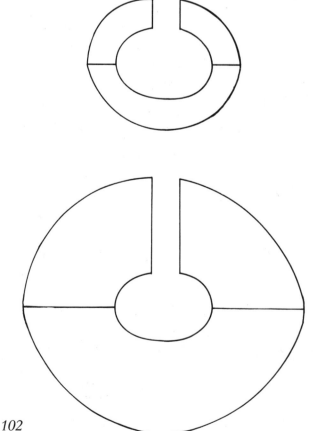

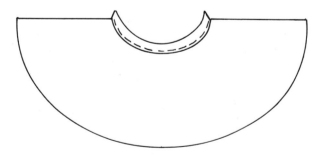

7-14. *After cutting out the dentalium shell base and dress neck facings, sew the shoulder seams.*

7-15. *Sew the dentalium shell base to the neck facings along the neck seam and understitch.*

seam. Run the needle and thread through the shell, stitch through the fabric at the bottom of the shell, run the thread behind the fabric, and bring the needle out near the neck seam for the next shell. Continue all around. (See Figure 7-16.)

Use the dark dots in the drawing as a guide to placing one-half of the sew-on snaps to the inside of the neck facing. Place the other half of the sew-on snaps to the inside of the garment in corresponding positions.

Snap the collar onto the basic garment and, starting at a corner at the back, fold under the seam allowance (cutting off interfacing as necessary) and blindstitch or slipstitch the collar to the garment near the zipper and around. (See Figure 7-17.) Finish garment following pattern.

Many Native American women, in addition to shells on the dress, add decoration to sleeve and dress bottoms. One example I have seen is a navy blue dress with a red 3-inch-wide (7.5-cm) band on sleeves and hem. You might prefer to add ribbons as hem decorations. Alternatively, to a navy blue dress, one might add rows of red, white, and purple ⅝-inch-wide (1.5-cm) ribbon, edge to edge, as one Native American woman did. The colors and widths of ribbons added are optional.

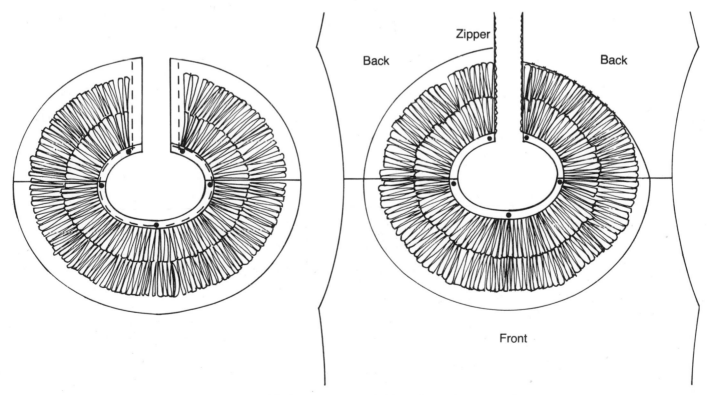

7-16. *Sew on dentalium shells and one-half of snaps, as indicated by dark circles on neck facings.*

7-17. *Blindstitch or slipstitch the dentalium-shell-covered base onto the dress.*

8 Northwest Coast Tribes Clothing Styles

FOR PURPOSES OF THIS BOOK, the Northwest Coast Tribes will refer to tribes living in the area along the Pacific Ocean, from Northern California to British Columbia, Canada. This whole coastline is lush with vegetation and, years ago, was abundant with game and ocean food. Inhabitants worked hard during the summer months to gather and preserve food. The food gathered in those few months was sufficient to feed the tribes for a whole winter. With winter months free, complex religions and cultures evolved. Fine crafts were also produced. The Northwest Coast Tribes are famous for their wood-carving skills. At one time, most artifacts of these tribes were made of carved cedar. All of these items were covered with carved decorations. Canoes, homes, storage boxes, bowls, spoons, and, of course, totem poles were heavily carved and often painted.

Weather permitting, Native American women of this area wore only a skirt, while the men wore nothing at all. The skirt was made of the worked bark of cedar trees. The women sometimes wore "blouses," which were rectangular pieces wrapped around the upper body or short, closed capes that were slipped on over the head. As protection against the rain and wind, both sexes donned a large,

knee-length cedar bark blanket. This was either thrown over the shoulders like a cape, wrapped around the body, or passed under one arm and over the other and tied or secured at the shoulder. Both men and women wore conical-shaped woven hats which were often decorated with painted Northwest-style designs.

To make clothing, most tribes used the bark of the red and yellow cedar trees. The bark was stripped from the trees, beaten, shredded, and then twisted into soft strings and woven into the needed garments. The "fabric" made from cedar bark was almost as fine as cloth and was similar in color to straw, though the yellow cedar tree bark was lighter than the red cedar tree bark. Some women dyed the fibers red using parts of the alder plant or a combination of fish eggs, crushed clam shells, and red rock.

These old costumes were well suited to the coastal country where a fine drizzle falls half the year. Tanned skin is useless in the rain; when wet, it stretches and tears and then dries hard. According to older tribe members, the cedar bark garments were excellent because they were extremely lightweight in addition to being water-resistant.

These cedar bark garments were worn into the nineteenth century as everyday wear by several coastal tribes. To prevent scratching, the edges of the robes were sometimes decorated with a strip of fur woven into the upper border.

An example of this garment is shown here. (See Figure 8-1.) This photograph was taken in the late nineteenth century and shows that some people wore the garment Pueblo style; that is, wrapped under the left arm and attached over the right shoulder.

While the majority of cedar bark robes were usually undecorated and served utilitarian functions, some robes were painted with designs and decorated with abalone and dentalium shells. (Both of these shells were highly prized objects. Abalone shell was obtained through trade from the California coast, and many hours were spent shaping it into circles and squares and drilling holes in it for buttons and jewelry. Dentalium was called the "money shell" and was used by some tribes as currency.) Sometimes leather was used for the decorated ceremonial robes. The decorated robes reflected the wealth of the owner and usually the designs on them were family crests. With the introduc-

8-1. *Many of the Northwest Coast tribespeople wore their cedar bark robes wrapped under the left arm and attached over the right shoulder in a fashion similar to the Pueblo women.* Courtesy Rare Book Division, The New York Public Library, Astor, Lenox and Tilden Foundations.

tion of trade goods, the Native Americans of the Northwest Coast replaced the painted cedar bark and leather robes with trade blankets decorated with flannel applique and rows of mother-of-pearl buttons. The blankets, called "button blankets," were worn on festive occasions for decorative value and for the prestige attached to owning so costly a garment. Most large button blankets are decorated with over one thousand buttons. (See Figure 8-2.)

Present-day use of designs on button blankets has changed, as these and other products are made for commercial sale. At one time, certain designs, usually representations of animals, were considered family crests and could be used only by members of the family who owned them. With the breakdown in culture and extended family structure, the use of designs is now less stringent. Present-day artists use Northwest-style designs as they choose, selecting them for their artistic appeal.

Contemporary button blankets are usually black or dark blue, although green and purple are sometimes seen. A red cloth border is added to the sides and top. The designs, usually of animals, are placed in the center. The designs may be produced in applique with red fabric and enhanced with one, two, or three rows of buttons, or they can be produced by using buttons alone with red applique accenting eyes and palms of hands and feet of the design animal. In addition, buttons can be used to edge the red borders or make other design additions on the border.

The wool blanket coat, also called a *capote,* was another garment popular in the Northwest Coast area, as well as in the Northern Plains, Rocky Mountains, and the Plateau areas. This coat, cut from a wool blanket, often with a hood, is one of the most practical and easily made articles of Native American style clothing.

Most tribespeople preferred the Hudson's Bay Company's blankets for their capotes. The white blanket with four colored strips at each end was most desired. White, tan, red, or green blankets with a dark stripe at each end were also popular.

Along with the broad colored stripes, some Hudson's Bay Company blankets have short black stripes, about 8 inches (20 cm) long, above the broad colored stripes. The short stripes are called "points," so a blanket might be called a four-point or a six-point blanket, depending on the number of short stripes. At one time, these points indicated the number of beaver skins required in trade for a

8-2. *This button blanket, made around 1890, sports a Thunderbird design which is recognizable by the feather plumes swirling from the back of his head.* Courtesy Portland Art Association.

blanket. A heavier, better-quality blanket required more beaver skins in trade. (Figure 8-3 shows a coat made of a three-point blanket.)

Also popular with Native Americans across the United States and Canada are Pendleton woolen blankets with brightly colored geometric designs. These are made by Pendleton Woolen Mills in Portland, Oregon. The blankets are particularly favored among Navajo, who wear them around the shoulders or carry them folded over the arm. Recently, a few Navajo women and women of other tribes have begun making coats for themselves from the geometric design Pendleton blankets.

Pendleton blankets come in different sizes and many different designs and colors. Among the Pendleton Com-

pany products, those with felt edges are considered men's blankets and those with fringed edges are for women. Apparently, the designs used by the Pendleton Company were not so much copied as inspired by Native American designs.

Pendleton also makes a blanket pattern called "Glacier Park," which is white with black, red, yellow and green stripes and is very similar to the Hudson's Bay Company product.

Northwest-Coast Cedar Bark Dress Adaptation

This dress is made of raw silk in a natural color that closely simulates the cedar bark worn by Northwest Coast Indians. The one-shoulder pattern copies one of the many ways the rectangular cedar bark robe was worn. Many of the Northwest Coast tribespeople liked to wear it wrapped under the left arm and secured over the right shoulder.

PATTERN

Use a commercial pattern for a street- or floor-length A-line dress with one shoulder. You may have to reverse the pattern so that the left shoulder is bare.

FABRIC

Use a coarsely woven fabric and one that has a visible crosswise weave, if possible. Raw silk and handwoven East Indian or Mexican cotton are suitable fabrics.

The color of the fabric should either be natural or reddish to approximate the cedar bark fabric used by the Northwest Coast tribespeople.

For a pattern similar to the one I used, a size 12, floor-length dress will require 3¼ yards (3 m) of 45-inch-wide (115-cm) fabric.

8-3. This coat is made from a "three-point" wool blanket. The points, which are short, black lines, can be seen just above the broad dark stripe on the left front of the coat. The owner traded three beaver skins to acquire the blanket. The seamstress who made the blanket into a coat added beadwork to the shoulders. Courtesy Denver Art Museum, Denver, Colorado.

8-4. *This modern "cedar bark" dress is made of raw silk fabric. The engraved silver necklace was made by a Northwest Coast artist.*

SPECIAL INSTRUCTIONS

Lay out and cut the fabric following the printed pattern instructions. Take extra care to use the reverse side of all the pattern pieces if your pattern needs to be reversed (so that the left shoulder is bare.)

The "Indianness" of this garment will be evident by the jewelry you wear with it. While it makes an excellent background for almost all types of Native American jewelry, it would be especially authentic to wear this garment with the engraved silver, gold, and copper bracelets, earrings, necklaces, and rings produced by Northwest Native American craftmen.

Northwest-Coast Button-Blanket Cape Adaptation

The lavishly decorated button blankets lend themselves easily to adaptation for contemporary wear. A cape embellished with the bold designs and colors can be stunning. The floor-length cape shown here required 502 abalone and mother-of-pearl buttons to enhance the thunderbird design. This number is only about half the number Northwest Coast tribespeople preferred on their button blankets.

PATTERN

The cape pattern should be a full one and either street- or floor-length. You may want to alter the pattern so that front red borders are sewn in, or you can applique the borders. For those who do not sew well, you can buy a full cape or other garment and add the borders and the design.

If you would rather produce a design on a skirt, use a wide, A-line, floor-length pattern. A jacket or vest with a design on the back is another possibility.

8-5. *The Northwest-Coast style of blanket decor was used to adorn a floor-length cape.*

111

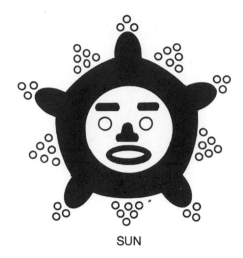

SUN

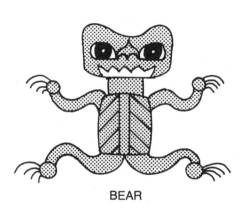

BEAR

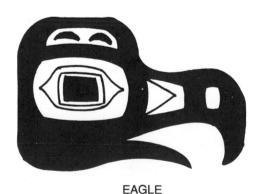

EAGLE

FABRIC

I suggest wool or wool blends. These are the fabrics used by most Native American women, and you need a fairly heavy, stable fabric to support the weight of the buttons. I also recommend black, dark blue, green, or purple, with red borders and applique as the colors. Applique in the design and fabric for the borders can be flannel, which many Native American women use, or wool or felt. One contemporary button-blanket maker uses red satin for the borders and lining.

A size 12, floor-length cape will require about 4½ yards (4.1 m) of 60-inch-wide fabric. One yard (.9 m) of 60-inch-wide red fabric should be sufficient for most large applique designs. Buy 1¾ yards (1.6 m) if you intend to add borders to front edges.

To be authentic you would use abalone and mother-of-pearl buttons as the Northwest Coast Indians did. These natural materials have a nice sparkle and reflect light better than do artificial materials. They are available from fabric and Native American crafts supply stores. However, contemporary examples of button blankets show heavy use of white plastic buttons; large abalone or mother-of-pearl buttons are used only for the eyes. Certainly plastic buttons are more readily available in the quantities you will need and are less expensive. Smaller ¼- to ½-inch-wide (.6- to 1.2-cm) buttons are used in the design and border. The abalone or mother-of-pearl buttons used for the eyes or accent on hands or wings can be from ¾ (1.8 cm) to 2 inches (5 cm).

Two-hole buttons take less time to attach. Buttons need not be exactly the same size or style. Examination of several Indian decorated blankets shows great variety in size and style, almost as if the maker had cleared out her spare button drawer. To give an idea of how many buttons you will need, the Thunderbird pattern on the cape shown, which is large and rather detailed, has 502 buttons. Also, I did not use any buttons to decorate the red borders on the front of the cape and most Northwest Coast seamstresses do enhance their borders to some degree.

SPECIAL INSTRUCTIONS

Lay out and cut the cape pattern pieces following the printed pattern instructions. If you want to add a red border along the two front pieces of the cape to simulate the borders on a true button blanket, it is best to alter the pattern. I marked and cut 2⅛ inches (5.3 cm) off the front pattern piece down the entire center front seam. Add ⅝-inch (1.5-cm) seam allowance to the cut edge of the cape and to the cut edge of the newly created border pattern piece. When cut out, my red border pattern piece was 2¾ inches (6.8 cm) wide, and 1½ inches (3.7 cm) of red border showed when it was sewn in. You may want to add a somewhat wider border.

It is best to work on the back piece before the garment is assembled. If there are two pieces in the cape back, as required by the cape pattern used for my cape, sew the center back seam.

Select your design from those given here or check books and museum show catalogs for a design you like. There are many books about Northwest Coast art that contain designs very suitable for enlarging. Once you have chosen your design, enlarge it and make a pattern from heavy paper. (To give an example of how much to enlarge your design, the Thunderbird on my cape measures 40 inches long and 36 inches at the widest part.)

Lay the paper pattern on the back piece of the cape to check proportion and positioning. If your cape pattern has a hood, the design should be placed somewhat low, so that when the hood is down, it will not cover the applique work.

Use the paper pattern to cut out the fabric applique piece and a piece of fusible web to entirely back the applique piece. The fusible web will prevent sags and bulges in the center of the applique piece. When working with a large garment, it is better to spread it out on the floor or on towels on a table rather than wrestle with it over an ironing board. With the fusible web in between the two, use your steam iron and a pressing cloth to fuse the applique piece to the cape back. Sew all edges of the applique piece using a zigzag stitch.

The bear motif (see Figure 8-6) can be used as described above or it can be used as a guide for placing an outline of buttons directly on the cape. Red applique pieces would then be used only for the eyes and mouth. To execute the outline, you will need to enlarge the design and make a paper pattern. Use a tracing wheel and fabric tracing or carbon paper to lightly mark the design on the fabric. Then use the marked outline as a guide for sewing on the buttons.

To estimate button placement, try laying out buttons on one small section of the design at a time. Space them

THUNDERBIRD

TREE OF LIFE (Cedar Tree)

8-6. *Designs from Northwest-Coast button blankets.*   *113*

8-7. *Alternative for button blanket border.*

from ½ to 1¼ inches (1.2 to 3.2 cm) apart, depending on the button size and your preference. Smaller buttons look better when placed close together. When satisfied with the look, remove the loose buttons and sew to the applique piece. Sew the buttons on the red applique piece, placing them near the edge.

Because the buttons will not be under any stress, it is sufficient to go through the holes only once (using quadrupled thread) and bring the thread behind the garment to the next button if sewing by hand. Many zigzag sewing machines have attachments for sewing on buttons and this makes the task go faster.

You may want to add more border decoration to your garment. The dotted area in the illustration shows where you would apply red border fabric, and the small circles show where buttons are to be attached.

Finish constructing the cape following the printed pattern instructions.

Northwest-Coast Blanket Coat Adaptation

This coat is adapted from the blanket coat so prevalent in the cold Northwest Coast and Plains areas during the nineteenth century. (See Figure 8-8.)

It is best to follow the Native American example and use a simple wrap coat pattern and a good-quality wool

8-8. *A wool blanket with geometric designs made into a coat.*

blanket. The coat is unlined and the edges are bound with felt. Wool blankets cost over fifty dollars, but, if made into a classic coat style, one will last for years.

PATTERN

Choose a commercial pattern for a wrap-style coat with either set-in or raglan sleeves. If you can find one, a pattern in which coat front and back are one piece and only collar and sleeves are separate pieces would be especially suitable to help preserve the geometric blanket designs. Pockets can either be inseam or patch style.

FABRIC

You will need one wool blanket, at least 64 by 80 inches (162 by 202 cm) and ⅛ yard (.11 m) of 60-inch-wide (150-cm) good-quality felt.

If you will be using a felt-edged wool blanket, buy felt in a color matching the felt on the blanket. The felt can be of any color if you are using the striped blankets. An alternative to felt for binding the striped blanket coat edges is ribbon.

The Pendleton felt-edged "man's blanket" is somewhat less expensive than the other blankets mentioned and the felt edges can be used for some of the edges of the coat. Patch pocket edges, if desired, can be finished with purchased felt to match the felt edges of the blanket.

Pendleton and Hudson's Bay Company blankets are available at department stores, some western wear clothing stores, some Native American jewelry and supply stores, and many trading posts on reservations.

SPECIAL INSTRUCTIONS

I used a Pendleton felt-edged blanket for my coat. The coat pattern requires several alterations. First calculate your desired finished coat length and cut off the hem allowances of the coat front and coat back. Calculate your desired finished sleeve length and cut away hem allowance. You will not need the hem allowances, because these cut edges will be bound with edge binding. Trim seam allowances from the front opening edge, including the lapels, if any, and all edges except the neck edge of the collar. The belt will be cut in two pieces. My belt pattern piece measured 2½ by 31½ inches (6.3 cm by 80 cm). My pattern had inseam pockets that did not require alteration.

Lay out the coat pattern pieces. Lay the hem lines of the sleeves, coat back, and coat front even with the felt edges of the blanket. The front edge seam line should also be even with the edges of the blanket.

Before cutting, carefully remove 16 inches (40 cm) of the felt edge binding above the front coat piece. Once you have attached the collar, you will reattach the felt edge binding around the collar, the ends meeting at the middle of the collar. This eliminates piecing felt edge binding on the coat lapels where it would be very noticeable.

Cut out the pattern pieces, being careful not to sever the extra felt edging extending from the top of the front lapels. Cut only one collar. You will not need an undercollar or collar facing.

Sew the coat fronts to the coat back along shoulder and side seams. Attach the sleeves. Place the right side of the collar toward the wrong side of the coat, neck edges even, and stitch. Press the seam open, trim the seam allowances to ¼ inch(.6 cm), and slipstitch the seam allowances open. When the collar is folded into its correct position, it will cover the open seam.

Starting at one lapel hand-baste the extra felt edging around to the middle of the collar. Do the same starting at the other lapel. Overlap the felt edges about ½ inch (1.2 cm) and cut off any excess felt edging. Stitch with your sewing machine.

You will have to create the belt from two pieces of fabric. Remove any felt edging from the cut belt pieces. Sew the belt pieces together, press the seam allowances open, turn under ¼ inch (.8 mm), and stitch the seam allowances flat. Cut strips of purchased felt into 1¼-inch (3.1-cm) widths and bind the edges of the belt.

If you are using a blanket other than a felt-edged one, you will still need to alter the pattern pieces as described above. If you choose a blanket with one stripe, the stripe should run around the lower part of the coat. The stripe on the sleeve can run either around the upper or lower arm. (Use Figure 8-9 as a guide to laying out the pattern pieces.) Cut out the pattern pieces. Sew coat fronts to back at the shoulder and side seams. Attach sleeves and collar as described above.

Use 1¼ inch-wide (3.1-cm) ribbon or felt strips. Press the edge binding in half. Bind collar, front edges, hem edges, sleeve bottoms, and the belt.

If your pattern includes patch pockets on the coat front, cut out the pockets after eliminating all seam allowances and top foldover allowances. Bind all edges with edge binding and sew into position, as indicated on the coat front pattern piece.

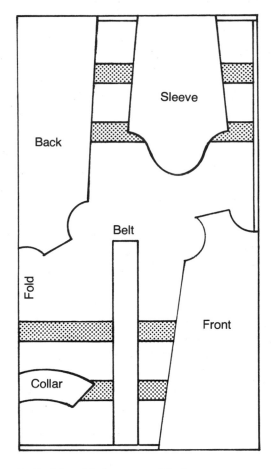

8-9. *Use this layout guide for coat pattern pieces, whether you are using a geometric design or striped blanket.*

117

9 Native American Design Fabrics

 FOR MANY YEARS, any mention of "Indian design motifs" brought to mind silhouetted images of teepees, buffalo, thunderbirds, and occasional crisscrossed arrows for many people. Recently, a few enterprising individuals have recognized the wealth of design motifs used for centuries by Native Americans in weaving, basketry, pottery, and beadwork. These people, some of Native American descent, have begun hand-printing cloth with attractive design motifs for sale by the yard. Shops selling these fabrics are located mostly in the Southwest. The designs being produced and sold are usually copyrighted. The following pages show fashions produced from these printed fabrics, and, at the end of this chapter, there is a short list of well-established businesses that sell these fabrics—some by mail.

Occasionally, a large company will produce a print that sells nationwide. In recent years, bed sheets printed with Native American style designs have been available. Material used for sheets is almost always permanently pressed, and dyes are selected for durability. Any garment made from sheets is likely to wear long and well. The only caution is that the print may be produced for a limited time only, so it is best to buy it when you see it.

Some words of warning concerning the use and care of hand-printed fabric are in order. Dye lots often vary from bolt to bolt, so it is important that you calculate carefully how much fabric you need. When working with border prints and overall patterns with varying pattern repeat intervals, extra fabric is needed. Because the dyes are delicate, special care must be taken when cleaning and pressing these printed fabrics. Often hand-washing in gentle

9-1. This two-color pottery print called "Rolling Rocks" has been made into a dress. The fabric is by Dendahl's of Santa Fe, New Mexico.
9-2. This long skirt is printed with a Pueblo pottery design called "Sityatka." The belt is a handwoven Pueblo belt. Maridadi West printed the prehistoric motif on homespun-look cotton.

suds is recommended and only certain methods of dry-cleaning are advisable. Pressing should be done on the wrong side or with a pressing cloth. Ask for special care instructions when purchasing any hand-silkscreened fabric. Considering the beauty and uniqueness of the garments that can be produced from these fine fabrics, this special care is worthwhile.

The dress shown here is made from a border-printed fabric created by Dendahl's, Inc. of Santa Fe, New Mexico. (See Figure 9-1.) The design is called "Rolling Rocks." The black and rust design is printed on natural color homespun cotton fabric. When working with such special fabric, choose a classic-style garment, such as this shirtwaist dress, so you can wear it for several years. Dendahl's still uses a lot of cotton and cotton-blend fabrics, but has in recent years perfected silkscreen printing onto good-quality polyester knit.

These printed fabrics can be made into casual or dressy garments. Shown here is a skirt of a natural color homespun cotton fabric. (See Figure 9-2.) The brown design, called *Sityatka,* is taken from a prehistoric pottery piece and was silkscreened onto fabric by Maridadi West, Inc. in Fort Collins, Colorado.

The tunic top shown is made of gray polyester and cotton blend fabric printed with black ink in the "Two Gray Hills" design. (See Figure 9-3.) The Navajo owned and operated Nizhonie, Inc. company in Cortez, Colorado, adapted this intricate pattern from the Navajo rug designs produced in the Two Gray Hills area of the Navajo Indian Reservation.

The fabric shown in the next photograph is unfortunately unavailable, but the outfit is a good example of how a small, overall print can attractively be made into a comfortable two-piece ensemble suitable for work or other daytime activities.

Fabrics printed with Native American designs are also very attractive additions to any home decor. Dendahl's recommends use of their printed fabrics for draperies, slipcovers, bedspreads, tablecloths, and napkins. Nizhonie, Inc. has drapery-making equipment in their workroom/sales office and offers a wide choice of fabrics and colors. They will print their designs any way you specify. Maridadi West, Inc. has in recent years expanded their printing of graphics on heavy cloth suited for hanging. A source list of Native American design printed fabrics is on page 122.

9-3. *This tunic top is made from a Nizhonie fabric in an overall print entitled "Two Gray Hills."*

9-4. *This print of Pueblo Indian symbols on cotton fabric has been sewn into an attractive two-piece ensemble.*

Sources for Native American Design Fabrics

Dendahl's, Inc.
P. O. Box 817
Santa Fe, New Mexico 87501

Dendahl's advertises hand-silkscreened authentic Indian designs. A brochure with designs in scale is available on request. There is an informal mail order service and custom work is done.

Maridadi West, Inc.
4300 W. County Road 50
Ft. Collins, Colorado 80521

A silkscreen process is used to produce prints of pottery and pictograph designs, as well as others with a Southwestern flavor. Brochures are available, custom work is done, and an informal mail order service exists.

Nizhonie, Inc.
P. O. Box 729
Cortez, Colorado 81321

Silkscreen process is used by the Navajo owners to produce numerous designs available in a variety of colors on different fabrics. A brochure is available upon request. A mail order service exists and custom work is done.

Pendleton Woolen Mills
Dept. N-924
Portland, Oregon 97201

This address is not for mail order. Write for a list of stores that sell Pendleton products.

The Bay
Mail Shopping Service
674 Granville Street
Vancouver 2, British Columbia, Canada

Write for a brochure and price list. Enclosed a self-addressed stamped envelope for quick reply.

Bibliography

NAVAJO

Conn, Richard. *Robes of White Shell and Sunrise: Personal Decorative Arts of the Native American*. Denver, Colorado: Denver Art Museum, 1974.

Minor, Marz Nono. *The American Indian Craft Book*. New York: Popular Library, 1972.

"Something about Navajo Dress." Window Rock, Arizona: Navajo Tribal Council, Navajo Parks and Recreation Department, no date.

APACHE

Conn, Richard. *Robes of White Shell and Sunrise: Personal Decorative Arts of the Native American*. Denver, Colorado: Denver Art Museum, 1974.

Douglas, Frederic H. *Indian Women's Clothing: Fashion and Function*. Denver, Colorado: Denver Art Museum Department of Indian Art, Leaflet 109, December, 1951.

PUEBLO

Conn, Richard. *Robes of White Shell and Sunrise: Personal Decorative Arts of the Native American*. Denver, Colorado: Denver Art Museum, 1974.

Douglas, Frederic H. *Basic Types of Indian Women's Costumes*. Denver, Colorado: Denver Art Museum, Department of Indian Art, Leaflet 108, December 1950.

Driver, Harold E. *Indians of North America. Second Edition*. Chicago: University of Chicago Press, 1969.

Feder, Norman. *Pueblo Indian Clothing*. Denver, Colorado: Denver Art Museum, Leaflet 4, 1930.

Roediger, Virginia More. *Ceremonial Costumes of the Pueblo Indians: Their Evolution, Fabrication and Significance*. Berkeley, California: University of California Press, 1941.

SEMINOLE

Bell, Ron. "Patchwork of the Seminole." *Whispering Wind,* Vol. 7 (January, 1974), 4–10.

Capron, Louis. "Florida's Emerging Seminoles." *National Geographic,* Vol. 136 (November, 1969), 716–734.

Capron, Louis. "Florida's 'Wild' Indians, the Seminole." *National Geographic,* Vol. 110 (December, 1956), 819–840.

Conn, Richard. *Robes of White Shell and Sunrise: Personal Decorative Arts of the Native American.* Denver, Colorado: Denver Art Museum, 1974.

D'Amato, Janet and Alex. *American Indian Craft Inspirations.* New York: M. Evans and Company, 1972.

Douglas, Frederic H. *Basic Types of Indian Women's Costumes.* Denver, Colorado: Denver Art Museum, Leaflet 108, December 1950.

Dudley, Taimi. *Strip Patchwork.* New York: Van Nostrand Reinhold, 1980.

Hofsinde, Robert. *Indian Costumes.* New York: William Morrow, 1968.

Jacobson, Oscar Brousse. *North American Indian Costumes.* Nice, France: C. Szwedzicki, 1952.

"Seminole Patchwork." *American Indian Hobbyist,* Volume VI (September–October, 1959), 2–18.

Seminole Patchwork. New York: Hearst Corporation, *Good Housekeeping,* 1966. (Available for purchase from Goodhousekeeping Sewing and Needlework Center, 959 Eighth Ave., New York, NY 10019. Ask for booklet GHN #732, 25 cents each plus postage.)

IROQUOIS

Dahanadisonkwe. "Native Dress and Design Among the Iroquoian People." *American Indian Crafts and Culture,* Volume 7 (May, 1973), 5–9.

Douglas, Frederic H. *Indian Women's Clothing: Fashion and Function.* Denver, Colorado: Denver Art Museum, Leaflet 109, December, 1951.

Fadden Ray (Aren Akweks). *Costume of Iroquois.* Onchiota, New York: Six Nations Indian Museum, no date.

Lyford, Carrie A. *Iroquois Crafts.* Washington, D. C.: U. S. Department of the Interior, 1945.

Wudarski, Don. "Iroquois Costume." *Whispering Wind,* Volume 7 (April, 1974), 5–13.

GREAT LAKES AREA TRIBES

Conn, Richard. *Robes of White Shell and Sunrise: Personal Decorative Arts of the Native American.* Denver, Colorado: Denver Art Museum, 1974.

"Indian Summer: Real Indian Gear." *Mademoiselle,* Volume 73 (June, 1971), 114–119.

"Ribbon Decoration." *American Indian Hobbyist,* Volume 3 (October–November, 1956), 12–23.

Ritzenthaler, Robert Eugene. *The Woodland Indians of the Eastern Great Lakes.* Garden City, N. Y.: Natural History Press, 1970.

"You Can Make These Traditional Native American Crafts," and accompanying booklet, *Redbook,* Volume 142 (March, 1974), 96–101.

PLAINS TRIBES

Conn, Richard. *Robes of White Shell and Sunrise: Personal Decorative Arts of the Native American.* Denver, Colorado: Denver Art Museum, 1974.

"Details of a Sioux Cloth Dress." *American Indian Hobbyist,* Volume IV, Numbers 5 and 6 (January–February, 1958), 50–51.

Douglas, Frederic H. *Basic Types of Indian Women's Costumes.* Denver, Colorado: Denver Art Museum, Leaflet 108, December, 1950.

Holm, Bill. "Plains Indian Cloth Dresses." *American Indian Hobbyist,* Volume IV, Numbers 5 and 6 (January–February, 1958), 43–51.

Hungry Wolf, Adolf. *Good Medicine: Traditional Dress Issue.* Fort Macleod, Alberta, Canada: Good Medicine Books, 1971.

NORTHWEST COAST TRIBES

"A Coat and Cape From Blankets," *Family Circle,* Volume 86 (March, 1975), 82–83.

Conn, Richard. *Robes of White Shell and Sunrise: Personal Decorative Arts of the Native American.* Denver, Colorado: Denver Art Museum, 1974.

Cook, Dora Sewid (Kwakiutl Tribe)
Director/Manager of the Kil Sli Native Arts and Crafts
store in Vancouver, British Columbia, Canada.
Private interview held at the Kil Sli store, July 31, 1975.

Eklund, D. E. "Pendleton Blankets," *Arizona Highways,*
Volume XLV (August, 1969), 40.

Holm, Bill. "Making a Blanket Capote." *American Indian
Hobbyist,* Volume 3 (September, 1956), 2–3.

"How to Make Indian Blanket Coats." *Ladies Home Journal
Needle and Craft* (Fall/Winter, 1973), 80–81.

Kroeber, A. L. *Handbook of the Indians of California.* Berkeley, California: California Book Company, Ltd., 1953.

Portland Art Museum. Portland, Oregon. *Native Arts of
the Pacific Northwest.* Stanford, California: Stanford University Press, 1949.

Underhill, Ruth. *Indians of the Pacific Northwest.* Washington, D. C.: U. S. Department of the Interior, 1945.

Index